TABLE OF CONTENTS

Top 20 Test Taking Tips

1. Carefully follow all the test registration procedures
2. Know the test directions, duration, topics, question types, how many questions
3. Setup a flexible study schedule at least 3-4 weeks before test day
4. Study during the time of day you are most alert, relaxed, and stress free
5. Maximize your learning style; visual learner use visual study aids, auditory learner use auditory study aids
6. Focus on your weakest knowledge base
7. Find a study partner to review with and help clarify questions
8. Practice, practice, practice
9. Get a good night's sleep; don't try to cram the night before the test
10. Eat a well balanced meal
11. Know the exact physical location of the testing site; drive the route to the site prior to test day
12. Bring a set of ear plugs; the testing center could be noisy
13. Wear comfortable, loose fitting, layered clothing to the testing center; prepare for it to be either cold or hot during the test
14. Bring at least 2 current forms of ID to the testing center
15. Arrive to the test early; be prepared to wait and be patient
16. Eliminate the obviously wrong answer choices, then guess the first remaining choice
17. Pace yourself; don't rush, but keep working and move on if you get stuck
18. Maintain a positive attitude even if the test is going poorly
19. Keep your first answer unless you are positive it is wrong
20. Check your work, don't make a careless mistake

Introduction to the CLEP Series

Your school requires you to take this CLEP Assessment in order to test the breadth and depth of your knowledge in a specified subject matter. Through CLEP Exams, you have the opportunity to earn credit or advanced standing at most of the nation's colleges and universities. Because the issuance of your credit ensures competence in the subject area it is important that you take studying seriously and make sure you study thoroughly and completely.

Principles of Macroeconomics

Basic Economic Concepts

Economics as a science

The study of economics includes microeconomics, which is concerned with smaller units, such as individuals and firms. and macroeconomics, which looks at the economy as a composite, taking a more global view. In general, economics deals with topics such as scarcity, supply, demand, and choices made by various parts of the economy and the total economy.

There are a variety of economic topics that overlap both microeconomics and macroeconomics. These hybrid areas may be covered separately or as a part of the micro/macroeconomic spectrum. Now called "mainstream" economics is a blend of macroeconomics and economic theory developed in the last 50 years. This includes a number of schools of economic thought, each with its own assumptions, conclusions, and methodology. Economics centers on the idea of scarce resources and how to best utilize these resources to meet the needs of individuals and the economic system as a whole.

The exchange of services and goods in an organized marketplace, where sellers and buyers vie to optimize their results by trading, is the mechanism where the study of economics occurs. Factors of production, the directed use of labor and capital, and the achievement of profit are the driving forces of an economic system. The clearest representation of these elements occurs in a free market economy, of which capitalism is the prime example. These factors are also in play in state-controlled systems which include communism and socialism. Many contend that in all economic systems the driving force is self-interest, or the "Invisible Hand" that Adam Smith defined in his Wealth of Nations.

Economics may be studied in a wide spectrum of political, social, and financial systems. Commonalities and contrasts may be used as a method of comparing economic theory in a variety of settings. Many of the crucial components of economics are active in any organized society, regardless of its philosophy.

Political economy was defined as the economics of competing states, and was the term used by early economic thinkers. Neoclassical economists discarded this term in the late 1800's in favor of simply "economics". the origin of the term "economics" is from the Greek meaning "settlement laws".

Economics was a recognized field in early Greek, Arab, and Roman eras. This is known as the "premodern"period. The mercantile and physiocrat systems are termed "early modern", and what we now call economics is named "modern economics" in the history of economic thought. The pioneers of modern economic thought include such giants as Karl Marx, David Ricardo, John Stuart Mill, and of course, Adam Smith. Economic references and problems are discussed in early texts such as the Old and New Testaments. Economic thought has often been important parts of political systems such as Communism and Socialism, and has played a major role in all societies.

History of economics

Ibn Kahldun of Tunis, writing in the 12th century, discussed political and economic theory. A favorite subject of his was population density and its effect on economic cycles. This is one of the earliest records of economic theory.

Scholasticism, a theological school of philosophy in the Middle Ages, incorporated a debate over a number of basic economic issues, including how a fair price of something could be determined. In the wars between the Church and her reformers during the Reformation, the concept of free trade arose and was considered in both a theological and political context.

The church and nobility saw economic activity as a way to raise revenues, and imposed taxes on almost all transactions. These taxes were used to finance wars and enrich the ruling classes, almost never benefiting those being taxed. Feudalism imposed its own system of economics, determining how most economic affairs would be reconducted and taxed. Needless to say, the serfs rarely saw any good from these measures.

The Mercantilists, a group of European importers and exporters, strived to profit from exploring new markets, trading goods at a profitable rate, and growing their markets. Mercantilists were the dominant economic force in the new state-nations of Europe. Their activities were instrumental in leading to the discovery and settlement of the New World.

The Physiocrats, a school of eco-philosophy active in France during the Enlightenment, were led by writers such as Anne Turgot and Francois Quesnay. Arguably, this was the first school or movement that viewed economics as a field unto itself. Many believe that modern economics was founded by the Physiocrats. Later thinkers and writers such as Adam Smith and David Ricardo built their theories on the foundation laid by the Physiocrats. As a group, the Physiocrats were short-lived, but their

impact was significant in the development of economic thought.

Modern economics

Modern economics is based on one basic premise - that resources are scarce and limited, and that choices must be made in the acquisition and use of them. All other questions and alternatives flow from this assumption. Economic choices involve sacrificing something in order to obtain another thing. This sacrifice is called the "opportunity cost" of the choice. I may choose to spend my last dollar on a candy bar rather than a writing tablet - thus the opportunity cost of the candy bar is the tablet. There are seemingly endless choices in a consumer society, all of which involve choices and opportunity costs. The choices and opportunity costs are expressed in price relationships in modern economics.

Each individual makes many economic decisions (choices) each day and the aggregate reflects economic activity of a society. Choices are driven by the utility, or want-satisfying abilities of the goods and services. Choices are ranked on the ability of the good or service to fill a perceived need of the individual. This utility function is active in most, but not all, economic choices.

Utility function and neoclassical economics

Neoclassical economists consider the utility function paramount in most economic and non-economic choices of individuals and states. This includes both short-term and long-term economics.

This theory of economic behavior extends to decisions made daily by consumers. What to consume and at what cost are the driving forces of microeconomics. Understanding that consumption choices involve opportunity costs is implicit in the economic choices made.

Neoclassical economists tend to favor what has been termed "supply side" economics, focusing on providing incentives to individuals and business rather than attempting to manipulate demand. Monetarism attempts to influence economic activity and growth through increasing or decreasing the money supply in an economy. Proponents of this philosophy tend to reject direct government intervention in the economy.

Economic schools of thought

Schools of economic thought may be loosely categorized as follows:

- 16th - 18th Century - Dominated by the European nation-states who pioneered Mercantilism in an effort to enrich themselves through trade and exploration of new markets. The Physiocrats were an important 18th century economic school that originated in France.
- 18th - 19th Century - Great economic thinkers and philosophers such as Adam Smith, John Stuart Mill, Thomas Malthus, and David Ricardo wrote important works that provided the foundation for Classical economics. This period also saw the rise of the "Utopian Socialists", who formulated economic ideas to cure the ills of society. Marxism is also included in this period although it mixes political social, and economic theory in a hybrid philosophy.
- Late 19th Century - Alfred Marshall is felt to be the father of Neoclassical economics. Marshall authored the concept of "marginal theory of value" which is the

cornerstone of Neoclassical economics.
- 20th Century - Carl Menger wrote the seminal work on economics for what was to be called the Austrian school. The American Institutionalist school and German school of economics appeared during this period.

Modeling and economic reasoning

The development of a methodology and logistical framework for discussion and argument has been an important step in the development of economics as a science. Modern economics has utilized new information gathering and processing technologies that expedite and organize the compilation of economic information. Much more detailed data is now available as the raw material for economic methodology.

The application of "Modeling" to economics has provided a framework for the application of the scientific method to economics, to study economic behavior and test hypotheses. Modeling allows the creation of artificial relationships to measure and manipulate economic activities. Models mirror the real world of economics, and provide an opportunity for economists to systematically study economic relationships.

As more sophisticated methods of study have evolved, the application of mathematics to economics, termed "econometrics", has yielded more accurate and useful information in economic methodology.

Microeconomic theory

The development of economic theory as it relates to individual units in a society is called microeconomics. These units may be individuals, firms, labor forces, resource pools, and consumers. The behavior of both people and businesses is included in microeconomics. The term itself means "small scale" economics. Microeconomics questions how the activities of small units in an economy interact, and the implications of such transactions. The utilization of scarce resources by individuals and firms is a central topic in microeconomics. Models of the marketplace where households and commercial companies interact and trade are key components in microeconomics. Economic activity is sometimes viewed as a process between corporations, businesses, and individuals. This process illustrates the mechanisms of a market economy when studied from small individual units within that economy. Relationships between scarce assets, such as natural resources, money, labor, and the factors of production are all easily visualized from the individual level of economics.

Trade between nations

Commerce between nations, the trading of products and service functions from one country to another, is called international trade. Trade between countries was very limited in the premodern era. As the capabilities for shipping and transport increased, so did the opportunities for international commerce. Today it constitutes a significant portion of many countries economies. The rise of companies doing business in many countries has contributed to the increase of international trade. The term "globalization", has come to mean the spreading network of connecting economic ties throughout the world. International trade is used as a political as well as economic strategy in relations between nations. As countries seek new markets in order to grow and prosper, international commerce is an ideal avenue for economic growth. Tariff policy is another weapon used in geo-

politics as nations strive to prosper in an increasingly competitive world. Economic success for many individual firms depends on their ability to develop international markets for their goods and services.

When international trade began to flourish under Mercantilism, countries protected themselves with high tariffs and restrictions on what and how goods might be traded. Over time, free trade was recognized as the most beneficial way to promote economic well being. This concept has been honored over the years (with some exceptions), and free trade remains the prevailing attitude in commerce between nations. In the modern economic era, treaties and agreements among countries has resulted in a more rigidly regulated international trade environment.

Free trade has historically favored nations with the strongest economies, and that remains the case today. The leading countries of the free world all advocate free trade, and developing nations have recognized the advantages in expanding their markets into the global economy. The future of free trade seems bright, and bodes well for a growing international business climate.

The primary risks in international trade are economic in nature. Care must be taken in international commerce to accurately asses the economic stability of the buyer. Trade partners must have confidence in the liquidity of their counterparts, and be assured that the buyer has the continued means to meet his obligations. This confidence fosters an atmosphere where international commerce can grow and flourish. Countries must believe that they have not lost control of their economic destiny by trading freely.

Another related area of concern in the geo-political arena. Economic policy is a powerful tool that may be used as a political weapon on occasion. Concerns about trading with potential enemys as well as possible confiscation during periods of international strife are real. Firms may become dependent on certain licenses to engage in international business, and fear the revocation of these agreements. The uncertainty of foreign exchange rates and stability of trading partners economies remain realistic concerns in today's global economy.

Balance of trade

Every country hopes to have a positive balance of trade. This means they have sold more goods and services abroad than they have purchased. Such a positive balance of trade (called a surplus) indicates a strong economy with good international markets. Conversely, a negative balance of trade (called a deficit) can indicate some fundamental weakness in a country's ability to profitably engage in international commerce.

Trade restrictions, including tariffs and other regulations, can weaken a country's trading position. Widely fluctuating exchange rates may cast uncertainty on the wisdom of trading with a particular country. Social and political environments have a direct effect on international commerce. Basic economic indicators such as inflation, price levels, and aggregate demand and supply all have a bearing on the balance of payments. Ultimately, it is the totality of all these issues that may determine the success of a country in international business.

Comparative advantage

Why would two countries continue to trade if one can produce goods and services cheaper than another? The answer is a comparative advantage, which depends upon the ratio between the costs of producing different products. This concept was introduced by David Ricardo in his seminal work on political economy and trade.

Essentially the principle states that each nation should specialize in producing the commodity with the lower opportunity cost. This would give the country a comparative advantage in exporting that product. It should trade with another country for a product for which it has a comparative disadvantage. Thus each country will benefit from buying goods abroad that are more costly to produce at home. Competitive advantage is the principle that makes international commerce work effectively. If a country does not have a competitive advantage in a product there must be other reasons for that country to trade.

Free trade and trade barriers

The exchange of goods and services across international boundaries can be termed "free trade" only if the traded products are untaxed and no restrictions apply. Trade barriers of one kind or another or tariffs make free trade impossible and are a deterrent to commerce between nations. Trade barriers may include taxes on imports, known as tariffs, limited amounts of a specific product that may be exported to a country, and other laws, restrictions, taxes or regulations limiting the unfettered commerce between countries.

Free trade is also promoted by economic policies that foster the movement of both labor and capital between countries. This climate of economic cooperation is needed to insure a working economic relationship between trading partners. Regional trade agreements or treaties often outline the rules and regulations of commerce between nations. A country cedes some of its economic independence when engaging in free trade . Their are both costs and benefits that must be assessed.

Historically, free trade has been an opportunity for a country to open and develop new markets to improve their economies. Free trade was largely unknown until the 15th century, and had grown steadily (but not without problems) over the decades. England, with a strong manufacturing economy, was a leader in advocating unfettered commerce among countries. The theory of free trade was included in the economic works of Adam Smith and David Ricardo.

Free trade has been a subject of contention over the years with different political, social, and economic systems resisting the concept. Protectionism, the policy of protecting economies against competitive imports, has been the main argument against free trade. Newly developing economies use protectionism to insure the success of their budding industries. As their economies mature and grow stronger, the pressure for new markets often makes free trade an attractive option.

Scarcity and choice

Economics could rightfully be called the study of scarcity. Limited resources are available to satisfy the wants and needs of both individuals and states. Economics involves the choices made by an economy to satisfy these wants and needs. Every economy must choose what goods and services to produce, how to produce them, and for whom they are intended. Limitations of the factors of production - land, labor, and capital, sometimes make these choices difficult.

When an economic choice is made, their is an "opportunity cost" implicit in the choice. The opportunity cost is what is given up by making a choice. If a country chooses to manufacture automobiles, it may not have the industrial capacity to produce tanks or aircraft. Thus, the economic choice to make automobiles involves the opportunity cost of not making tanks or aircraft. Individuals and countries continually make economic choices and sacrifice opportunist costs in the process. An individual may choose to attend a film rather than go out to dinner. Choices are driven by what people and countries feel is in their best interest.

Supply and demand

A competitive market is composed of buyers and sellers engaged in trade in an organized manner. Price and the amount of products sold are determined by the supply of and demand for the goods or services. Microeconomics is the study of these market factors to understand and predict market activity.

A central tenant of the market is when demand exceeds supply of a good or service, the price will rise. However, when supply exceeds demand for a good or service the price will fall. The constant flux of demand, supply, and price always tends toward equilibrium - when supply and demand equal each other. In real economic systems, this point is rarely reached, and if so, only briefly. In a complex economy, where there are endless choices to be made, demand and supply only occasionally reach an equilibrium. Elements of economic choice and the opportunity cost of such choices make it very difficult for demand and supply to be equal for a particular good or service.

Market equilibrium

The condition of market equilibrium is achieved when demand for a good or service equals the amount of that product made available by suppliers. Any organized market tends to work toward a state of equilibrium, as the forces of supply and demand fluctuate over time. Shortages may occur, causing increased demand and higher prices. The higher prices will reduce demand, causing prices to drop as the market moves toward equilibrium.

In actual fact, the equilibrium point is rarely, if ever, attained, since the endless changes in supply, demand, and fluctuating prices create some imbalance between supply and demand. Despite this reality, it is important to note that a free market is always working toward this equilibrium state. The economic behavior of buyers and sellers will move the market in the direction of balance between demand and supply.

Shortages

When a good or service is demanded in excess of the ability of the supplier to meet this demand, a shortage will occur. A shortage will drive the demand of a product or service up, and prices will rise. Shortages can be artificially manufactured by suppliers to manipulate the market. An example of this occurred in the 1970's when OPEC chose to limit the production of oil in order to increase demand, and thus raise prices. This proved to be an effective strategy as Americans who depended on gasoline increased demand and prices rose because of the shortage. When OPEC increased the production of oil after political pressure was applied, supplies of gasoline returned to normal and prices fell. The market again moved toward equilibrium as the artificial manipulation of the supply of oil ended. This episode drove home the point that to depend on a few suppliers of a necessary product leaves consumers open to manipulated shortages.

Concept specialization

Labor, a major factor of production, must be used in the most efficient manner to optimize the economic system. The concept of specialization requires that labor (and other factors of production) be used on work at which they are most efficient in order to produce goods in the most cost-effective manner. This means allocating specific specialized operations to various members of the work force so each can concentrate on what he or she does best. The result should be an increase in productivity with a corresponding increased profitability of the firm.

When this concept is extrapolated throughout an economy, it provides a country with a competitive advantage, that is to say a nation, company, or individual will be producing most efficiently, giving a boost to productivity. Such an economy will tend to have an edge in international trade, and function more efficiently in the domestic economy.

Markets

Markets may be located physically in particular places, such as a produce market, or may be intangible, as a market for fine art. All markets operate under an implied agreement between buyers and sellers on trading for goods and services at specified but fluctuating prices. Markets provide the laboratory where economic theory and practice may be observed and studied. Anywhere that goods are offered for sale and buyers exist, a market is said to be present.

A specialized type of market is one in which all products are the same, and everyone has equal access to market information. Such a market is said to be perfectly competitive when it reaches a significant size. The size must be large enough that individual units of the market (buyers and sellers) are unable to

- 12 -

determine the price of the goods or services by themselves. In such a market, perfect competition may be said to exist. Practically, perfectly competitive markets are uncommon, due to myriad factors that affect a given market.

Market and command economy

When individuals own, operate, and control all factors of production, this is said to be a market economy. Everyone in a market economy strives to make a profit regardless of their activity. Entrepreneurship is the force that fuels a market economy. Market economies provide for more freedom of action among members, and these actions are guided by self-interest. Capitalism, including the private ownership of the factors of production, is the hallmark of a market economy.

Market economies are successful in part due to increased individual freedom for its members. When people have the freedom to make their own decisions, the economy is more likely to function efficiently. This is because changes in the markets will be noticed and responded to quickly and appropriately. There is more flexibility for economic action in a market economy system. Through private ownership and individual freedom, market economies, are the most successful systems for the operations of free markets in the world. The largest market economies today are the United States, Great Britain, and Japan.

A command economy is one in which the government controls basic economic activities. Such an economy is directed by decisions of one group (the ruling class) for all members of the society. Such a system, typical in dictatorships, suffers because of the lack of private interest in economic success. Command economies are slower to respond to changing economic fluctuations as they are

controlled by cumbersome organizations and not responsive to the "guiding hand" of self interest. Socialism and communism are examples of command economies today.

Price and price theory

A free market depends on a system of value to measure the scope and action of an economic system. Price is the traditional measurement of value between sellers and buyers in a market. Price theory measures the relationship between prices and other economic variables in a market economy. Price theory has demonstrated the importance of prices on both demand and supply in economic analysis. The demand for resources is a derived demand, based on demand for the products that require the resources for their production. The greater the demand for the final products of the resources the higher the price of those resources. Thus resources are priced just as goods and services are priced - according to the demand and supply for the resources. It follows that the price of final goods and services depends in large part on the price of the resources needed to supply the final product.

Price discrimination

When a supplier of the same goods and services uses a multitier price schedule to sell to different buyers price discrimination exists. Airlines provide a prime example, selling services for the same flight at many different prices depending on purchase date, age of the buyer, days traveled, and many other factors. Price discrimination is an economic strategy designed to increase economic profitability in a mixed market. It does not mean unfair or illegal manipulation of prices.

Sometimes a reverse price discrimination occurs, when a supplier charges the same price to different buyers, although the costs of the supplier to do so differ. One would imagine that price discrimination could only occur if a supplier held a monopoly; however in a complex economy with a so many pricing factors and decisions at work discrimination in pricing occurs almost everywhere. Sometimes this variation in prices can help lower prices for consumers, but this is not always the case.

As everyone who purchases tickets on an airline, price discrimination is rampant. The same flight from San Francisco to New York may offer a bewildering number of prices based on such factors as:

- Length (number of days) of the trip.
- Age of the traveler.
- Day of the week traveled.
- Purchase date of the ticket.
- Number of stops enroute to destination.
- Special fares and discounts not available to all travelers.
- Class of service offered on the flight.
- Flexibility of ticket.

Airlines sell into both business and vacation travel markets, and often differ their prices significantly. The success of on-line internet travel agencies has highlighted the price discrimination for airline tickets. A quick glance at one of these websites will show multiple examples of airline price discrimination.

Value

Value is the key economic element that drives many business decisions. Unfortunately, value may be difficult to define, meaning different things to different people. It is, however, the measurement by which utility, or want satisfying power may be defined. Some classical economists, including Adam Smith, tied labor to value, postulating that true value was the amount of work it takes to produce a good or service for sale. Although this is one legitimate manner in which to measure value, it is not the only one. An exception would be the relative ease of "making" emeralds, compared to the complexity of producing aircraft. The element of scarcity is also a vital component of the value of a good or service.

Some market theorists claim that price itself tells the value of a good or service. They They believe that countless economic variables are factored into determining a price for a specific good or service, and this price equals the value. In some sense value is a determinant of the individual's belief in the want satisfying power of any good or service.

Marginalism

Marginalism concerns itself with the economic worth of the last (or next) product or service provided. The cost of making the last product, the cost of hiring the last employee, the cost of selling the last product, determine the marginal cost of that next good. Presumably, a company will continue to produce goods and services until it becomes unprofitable. Production will cease when the marginal return of a product does not yield a profit.

From the point-of-view of the consumer, the marginal utility of the purchase is the crucial factor. How much want-satisfying power does an individual get from each purchase? When this marginal utility decreases too much, the buyer will not buy the next unit. The idea of diminishing returns often determines how much a buyer will purchase of a good or service. For example, after eating a piece of pie, the want-satisfying power of the next piece of pie will be less. When this marginal utility reaches a certain point, the consumer will stop buying.

Opportunity cost

The opportunity cost of an economic decision is always the cost of what opportunity is sacrificed by making that decision. For example, a person may have enough money for a vacation in Europe, or enough to purchase a new automobile, but not both. The opportunity cost of buying the automobile will be the trip to Europe. These decisions are made usually on the utility of each choice - which would provide the most pleasure to the consumer. In a complex economy, there are many competing factors that provide utility. An individual, firm, or government will always choose what they perceive to be the choice that will be most beneficial given limited resources.

These choices are usually not clear-cut and many factors go into some economic decisions. This is more common when companies or governments have to choose between a number of needed and attractive choices. Different parts of society or firms will have much different ideas about the best way in which to utilize their resources.

Price elasticity

When a price is changed, either increased or decreased, there will be a change in the demand for the goods and services. The rate at which demand falls or rises is called the price elasticity of demand. This measurement is usually formulated as a ratio of the changing price and the change in demand. If a price is raised by 20%, and demand falls by 20%, the ratio between them is the price elasticity of demand.

Normally, any rise in price will decrease the demand for the goods and services

offered. Any decrease in price should raise demand barring other external factors. This theory of price elasticity works best as a model, because in the real economic world there are a huge number of variables that affect price and demand. Usually businesses will test these variables to determine how much a price change will by itself affect demand.

If the demand of a good or service is affected by the change in price of a different good or service, cross elasticity of demand is at work. This is most often expressed as a ratio between the change in demand for the first good as the price of the second good fluctuates.

An example of this would be the change in demand for subway tickets in New York if the price of each ticket were to be doubled. The ratio between the drop in demand for use of the subway and the amount of the price increase would be the cross elasticity of demand.

The demand for a good or service is related to the income of prospective buyers of the good or service. Changes in the income of prospective consumers are measured in a ratio to the change in demand caused by the income change. If the income of a buyer pool increases 10%, and the demand for the product increases 10%, that ratio (1) is the income elasticity of demand.

The price of a good or service directly affects the quantity of supply of that good or service. The ratio between the price increase or decrease and the amount of the good or service supplied is called the price elasticity of supply. For example, a raise in the price of carrots will cause an increase in the supply of carrots as farmers produce more of that crop to increase profits. This price elasticity of supply is expressed as a ratio between the increase or decrease in price and the increase or decrease of supply.

If the price of carrots rises on the open market by 10%, and the supply of carrots increases by 10% the price elasticity of supply would be expressed as the ratio between these changes (1). Note that inventories of goods already produced will be a factor in determining the price elasticity of supply. Over the long run economists equate goods produced with goods supplied.

Surplus

A consumer surplus arises when prices fall and buyers realize extra savings which go into a surplus of buying power for purchasers. If for any number of economic factors, suppliers are able to sell at higher prices than they would ordinarily obtain, a supplier surplus exists.

In many areas, particularly commodities and farm products, governments intervene which may cause an artificial surplus. This government intervention usually takes the form of subsidies of some kind, and often represents the government holding a significant surplus itself. Taxes are another area of government intervention that can cause a surplus.

When all the existing surpluses in an economy are aggregated, the sum may be called the total surplus. Welfare economics uses this figure when they consider a consider a new policy, or to examine an existing one.

Individual demand curves

A demand by consumers or buyers is analyzed based on the ability of any good or service to satisfy the needs of that group. When all economic considerations are in play, including the price of a good or service and the amount supplied, consumers will, in general, choose the economic decisions that most fulfill their wants and needs. When all of these individual preferences are analyzed, the total pattern will represent aggregate demand curves.

Although each individual will operate to fulfill his or her needs as a separate unit, the aggregate of the total economy may differ. Social programs, tax incentives, and transfer payments will change the pattern of wealth distribution for the entire economy. Society as an entity may have a different aggregate demand than any individual. Since there is always a broad spectrum of wants and needs in any given society, the market cannot give a "greatest good for the greatest number" with any certainty.

Consumer preference

Microeconomics is concerned with individual decisions that ultimately affect the entire economy. Consumer behavior is an important aspect of microeconomics. Consumer preferences are difficult to assess, because of the seemingly endless choices, conscious and unconscious, that motivate consumer behavior. Economic models have been constructed to better understand consumer activities. These are sometimes called preference relations (charting consumers' preferences).

These models of consumer preferences have many flaws, but they can be used to attempt to predict the behavior of buyers under various sets of conditions. A major flaw may be termed the completeness of understanding consumer behavior. Although a preference model may be able to show in theory how consumers will behave under a set of economic conditions, it is impossible to measure all the factors that enter into choices made by buyers. These choices are subject to rapid change due to external economic changes.

Revealed preference theory

Predicting the buying patterns by consumers can be measured by the "Revealed Preference" theory, first articulated by Paul Samuelson, author of a best-selling economics textbook and a leading figure in contemporary economics. Samuelson postulated that the actual past buying habits could be used to analyze and predict future consumer activity.

Samuelson posited that if a consumer purchases a certain brand of ice cream, he or she will continue to do so until something changes his or her mind. Such a change might involve ice cream prices, better quality ice cream available as a competitor, discontinuation of a favorite flavor or brand, and a host of conscious and unconscious variables. The consumer may decide to lose weight, and give up ice cream as a staple of his or her diet. It can readily be seen that determining these consumer preferences have limitations since all factors involved in consumer decisions are impossible to know. Even so, revealed preference theory provides a base from which economists can study purchasing habits of individuals.

Indifference curves

Indifference curves are another example of a microeconomic tool that measures consumer activity. Indifference curves graphically display points on a spectrum where consumers are indifferent to a choice between two products. An indifference curve showing an individual's preference for, say, shirts, might indicate that the desire for a polo shirt and a turtleneck shirt were identical. Thus, both the polo and turtleneck shirts would all be located on the same point of the indifference curve.

Indifference curves were introduced as microeconomic tools by economists early

in the 20th century. It stemmed from the understanding that satisfaction of consumers could be accurately measured. This was called "cardinal utility". The new concept uses the principle of "ordinal utility", relying on individual economic decisions that could be objectively observed and analyzed, contrasted, compared, and become the basis for future predictions. From this graphical presentation of data, economists hope to better understand past consumption patterns and future buying activity.

Utility

Utility is a technical economic term that seeks to measure the want satisfying power of goods and services purchased by consumers. Everyone rationally attempts to increase their utility, that is to say, fulfill their satisfaction gained by economic choices. All goods and services may be measured on an economic scale, for an individual or firm that rates the utility of that product. Consumer choices (and all microeconmic choices) are made to increase overall utility for that entity. Some goods and services have increasing utility, the ability to better satisfy the individuals needs. Others have decreasing utility, less effective as want satisfying products.

Utility is combined with other economic tools such as indifference curves to attempt to measure and predict consumer behavior. Utility is also an important feature of welfare economics, where it is used to attempt to create the most satisfaction for the most people in an economy. The concept of utility as an economic tool was pioneered by Jeremy Benthan in the 17th century as an aspect of political economy.

Economists have striven for centuries to improve the economic position of society as a whole. This goal spurred economists to attempt to measure utility in a meaningful way, in order to maximize it for society. If utility could be measured for an individual, it was postulated that the aggregate utility for society could be measured. This was called cardinal utility. The problem with attempting to measure cardinal utility is the difficulty of measuring utility without an objective means of analyzing the information. Each individual has a different set of needs and wants and comparing a products utility between a diverse group is impossible.

Cardinal utility was abandoned as a useful tool in economics, and replaced by the concept of ordinal utility. Ordinal utility applied the scientific method to utility by observing patterns of prior economic behavior, comparing economic variables, and postulating predictions of future activity. This has proved a more valuable approach in economic analysis.

Marginal utility is founded on subjectivity, rather than objectivity. Marginal utility places its focus on buying and selling transactions between individual units in the economy, to the exclusion of the activity of the economy as a whole. the market place is the holy grail for the proponents of marginal utility, who see the markets as the foundation of economic activity. The production function is ignored, a crucial error as costs of production are a major determinant of prices, and therefore all microeconomic activity.

Critics of marginal utility say it is impossible to understand consumer utility, which is determined by prices in part. The prices themselves are based on consumer preferences, making an accurate analysis difficult if not impossible. Another area of criticism for the concept of marginal utility is that it often attempts to correlate utility with price. This correlation does not hold true where a product may be useful and

necessary to an individual, but be free. An example of this would be water.

Theories of value

Placing value on goods and services has been a problem concerning economists for centuries. Many scholastic and scientific arguments of the reformation period focused on the definition of value. The classical argument of value is illustrated in the "diamond-water paradox". It is pointed out that in comparisons of these goods, water is essential to life and either free or available at a low price. Diamonds, on the other hand are an unnecessary luxury and are very expensive.

Classical economic thinkers claimed that value could only be measured as the cost of production of the product. The difficulty and expense of making a good available imputed it with intrinsic value. Both Adam Smith and David Ricardo promulgated this theory of value.

Another school of thought on determining value stated that the value of anything was completely subjective. Nothing is valuable in and of itself, and only the perceived value imputed by the consumer is valid. This school, called the subjective theory of value, asserted itself in through the 20th century.

Income

Income, in common parlance, is the compensation received by economic units during the normal activities of business. This includes monies received from multiple sources including employers, investments, and gifts.

In the business world, gross income is the amount a company earns before expenses. Net income is the money the company has earned after paying the costs of doing business. A company's

- 18 -

revenue flow starts with monies received from goods and services sold to consumers. From this amount must be subtracted all monies spent in the operations of the business. This includes employees' salaries, costs of production, fixed and variable costs of doing business, and any intangible costs. The resulting figure is the firm's income (or loss). If a profit is made, this may be paid as additional compensation to owners, appropriate tax levies, or reinvested to improve the company's position in some respect. Publicly held corporations may choose to pay their stockholders a dividend.

The calculation of per capita income is made by taking the total of all monies earned by residents of a particular area divided by the number of inhabitants of the region. Note that per capita income is based on where the individuals live, rather than where they actually physically work. The aggregate of all monies is called Total Personal Income. This figure includes all earnings paid to individuals, transfer payments (social security for example), and investment income from all sources. the relative economic health of a particular area can be measured in part by per capita income and Total Personal Income.

Passive income is also accounted for in Total Personal Income. These are monies derived from rents, private portfolios of stocks and bonds, earned interest from any source, and various payments from pension funds and other employee retirement programs.

Another class of income is derived from government transfer payments. These include various social and disability benefits, as well as compensation for the unemployed.

Efficient market theory

Capital markets work under a different set of principles than do other markets. The market for stocks and bonds is an example of a capital market. Fama's "efficient market theory" attempts to describe the forces that operate in capital markets. According to this theory, the price of an equity security or bond is determined by an overall objective assessment of its perceived value after all information regarding the security is available and taken into account.

This theory is accurate only in theory because it assumes all information about the security is accurate (very rarely true), and that all individuals receive the information at the same time (almost never true). Additional assumptions that all relevant information arises spontaneously and the market is broad enough that no small group of individuals can manipulate the price. Sometimes called the "random walk theory," it claims any attempt to forecast market prices based on mathematical calculations or market analysis is futile.

Market failure

The term "market failure" has several definitions in economics. At the most basic level it means the market is unable to provide a stable trading framework for the distribution of goods and services to the buyers. In this case the market does not truly function under the economic definition of a trading exchange. Another way of viewing market failure is the common situation where the market is so grossly inefficient it simply malfunctions. Social welfare economists would deem any market that did not place the good of the society above all other factors as a failure.

In trying to understand the mechanics of market failure, economists have created models to study the phenomena. They believe market failure is often the result of errors in pricing based on faulty market research. Inaccurate information in setting prices can be a major cause of failure. Perhaps the major cause of market failure is the failure to adequately understand the nuances of the particular market involved.

Information asymmetry

In any economic transaction, a party with superior information commands a great advantage. When this is the case, information asymmetry is said to exist. An example would be the seller of a home knowing certain structural weaknesses that the buyer does not know. Frequently, sellers have more information because they are privy to details about their own property. Occasionally buyers may have the advantage in knowledge.

Information asymmetry allows dishonest sellers to sell inferior or sub-standard products to buyers who are unaware of the information. In a market with broad information asymmetry, the value of all products in the market, good and bad, may decline because of the lack of trust by buyers. If the situation is too commonplace, the market will fail. Knowledgeable consumers will no longer be willing to participate in such an unfair market.

Measurement of Economic Performance

Production

The production function in microeconomics refers to the total process of producing or assembling goods and services that are to be traded in a marketplace. Production decisions are some of the most vital in microeconomics. A firm or individual must decide what to make, and how many units to provide. This will often depend on the method of production and the unit price of making each product. An evaluation on the necessary resources to be utilized in another important production decision.

In tandem with sophisticated market research, optimum decisions can be made about producing goods and services.

Production is a process, and as such it occurs through time and space. Because it is a flow concept, an important statistic is the amount of production for a specific period of time. Other factors of concern are the amount and physical dimensions of the finished process. This will be important in storing and shipping the finished goods.

Efficiency and x-efficiency

The measurement of the productivity of a production process is vital. Productivity may be said to be efficient when the optimum number of finished products is produced with a minimum of raw materials, assuming quality control is maintained. If a production operation is less productive than anticipated, due to internal or external forces, it is said to be X-efficient. Such X-efficient production operations are often due to a number of factors beyond the control of the producer. Examples would be shortages of raw materials, increased and unexpected competition, or problems in the supply of necessary labor.

The productivity of a production function is simply based on how many units of a finished product can be made from a minimum amount of inputs. The more efficient processes give firms an important competitive position and greater flexibility in pricing and marketing. Decisions made about production will often determine the success or failure of the product line for a firm.

Factors of production

Factors of production are the sum total of the resources needed to produce finished goods. The major factors identified by economists include the use of land (for factories and agricultural products), labor (the human work force), natural resources (raw materials used in manufacturing), and capital goods (previously manufactured equipment used in production). Human inputs such as management and human relations could be added to the mix. Contemporary economists often include technological expertise into the factors of production.

Factors of production may be fixed (one which cannot be changed), or variable, which can be adjusted by management easily. Examples of fixed factors would be physical plants and heavy machinery. Any factor that can be easily manipulated by the "long run" all of these factors of production can be adjusted by management. The "short run" however, is defined as a period in which at least one of the factors of production is fixed. A fixed factor of production is one whose quantity cannot readily be changed. Examples include major pieces of equipment, suitable factory space, and key managerial personnel. A variable factor of production is one whose usage rate can be changed easily.

Diminishing marginal returns analysis

As additional raw materials are resources are added to production factors, a point occurs where the production function becomes less efficient. In other words, additional resources are yielding less profitable final products. This point is called the point of diminishing returns and is measured as a position on the marginal physical production curve. Continuing production will eventually result in producing products that lose money. Thus, it would be preferable to stop production.

Diminishing marginal returns will vary from industry to industry depending on the necessary factors of production needed to produce goods and services. The combination of land, labor, and capital needed for production is different for each product, so the point of diminishing marginal return will also differ. Demand, supply, and price changes in the factors of production will all impact this analysis.

Production functions

Production functions, an important area of analysis in microeconomics, concerns itself with the ratio of raw materials or resources needed to produce a certain amount of goods and services. This relationship may be depicted as a mathematical one or illustrated with a graph. The goal of analyzing the production functions is to optimize the amount of finished goods that can be obtained from the minimum of inputs. Many factors enter into such an analysis, including supply and demand of the factors of production, state-of-the-art technology, and managerial skill. Every production function will be different because of the mix of factors for producing different goods at various times.

If a producer knows the exact quantity of finished goods he or she must manufacture, the production function would be the minimum necessary resources needed to achieve that production number. Current technology will affect this combination of resources. In this type of analysis, costs and prices are not considered.

Controversy has surrounded the validity of production function analysis. Most of the criticism is concerned with the manner in which certain factors of production were measured, and the manner in which proportions of the factors were mixed.

Some economists feel it is not possible to post a necessary amount of capital without a complete understanding of both interest rates and the cost of labor. The production function analysis must include specific prices for all factors of production, but the analysis itself depends on knowing these variables. This is the "which came first the chicken or the egg" problem. Exact variables cannot be known until the production function analysis is complete, but the analysis is the method of determining the variables. Special mathematical constructs and assumptions must be built in these models of production functioned to have a useful function.

Production possibility curve

When any product is made, there is an opportunity cost of forgoing using the resources to make a different product. If two or more items are being produced at the same time, there will be opportunity costs involved in decisions regarding the relative amount of each product to produce. This analysis is called the production possibility curve.

The production possibility curve is a valuable tool for manufacturers because it explores production alternatives and their economic result. Points of maximum productivity may be plotted using this graphical tool, and it will also illuminate when production becomes inefficient. Companies can then choose optimum mixes of products as well as determine when a finished good is not economically feasible to manufacture. The analysis should yield the necessary information for a firm to adjust their product mix and quantities of goods produced to the most profitable level.

Economic rent

In economics, "economic rent" is a technical term that defines the ratio between the cost of a factor of production, and the revenue yielded by that factor. The utilization of each factor of production involves an opportunity cost which must be evaluated by a company. Choices the firm makes will decide on the optimal use of these factors in light of income received. A company must make decisions that select the processes which best optimize the productivity of that firm. A technical distinction may be made between economic rent and profits, because business entities often manufacturing and capital equipment and derive multiple benefits from them. Profit is a narrower concept, which may be calculated easily by subtracting business costs from business income. The two may be substantially different, depending on the organization of a company, ownership of capital goods, and the method of accounting used. Economic rent is a more theoretical term, while profit and loss, are practical indicators of the success or failure of a business.

Economies of scale

Economies of scale is an economic concept that measures the effects of the increase in production of a given product. Economies of scale refer to the changing variables that must occur when production is increased or decreased. The goal of this economic measurement is to determine the most ideal size of a company to maximize productivity and decrease inefficiency. Many factors enter into this concept including the available labor force, size of the physical plant necessary, cost and availability of raw materials, and managerial expertise to mix and balance these elements in the most effective manner. Ultimately, economies of scale are used to increase productivity and profit, the two measurements that are vital to the success of a firm. Diseconomies of scale indicate when production changes have reached a point where they are detrimental to the firm. This can be valuable information as companies plan production strategies and levels.

Economies of scope

Economies of scope are primarily concerned with the planning and implementation of product mix as a strategy of marketing and distribution. Economies of scale deal with the amounts of goods and services supplied, while economies of scope are more concerned with the types and numbers of different products the firm markets. An example would be a candy manufacturer deciding to introduce a new variation of an existing candy bar. Marketing and distribution channels would remain the same, name recognition would be present, and the product would fit nicely into the overall product concept of the firm. Should the company decide to add shoes to its line, diseconomies of scope become evident. Marketing strategy and distribution agencies would be different, as would packaging, storing, and shipping the final product. Such diseconomies of scope place major barriers in the path of product expansion into new and uncharted markets.

Economies of agglomeration

There are important benefits to be gained when companies follow a strategy of locating themselves physically close to each other. This strategy and the benefits it yields are called "economies of agglomeration." Most commonly used in urban areas, where multiple similar firms operate, economies of agglomeration is useful in various ways. It provides for a network effect valuable in efficiency in receiving raw materials, drawing from experienced labor pools, and creating competitive advantages in many ways.

This is true whether the companies grouped together are complementary or competitive. Both suppliers of raw materials and potential buyers will find it more convenient to work with companies that are physically near each other. Some areas, such as "silicon valley", are associated with particular industries.

Diseconomies of agglomeration also exist when firms group close together. Buyers may shop competitively more easily in a small geographic area. Numerous plants and manufacturing operations can degrade the quality of life in an area. A balance of these factors usually occurs in most modern urban areas.

Ideal firm size

Determining the optimum size for a company provides a challenge for managers. since businesses are measured in large part by profitability, the size of a firm should ideally be that which provides the greatest profit. This size will vary greatly between various companies, industries, and geographical locations. The ideal size of a firm is a fluid variable, changing with economic and competitive fluctuations. Economies and diseconomies of scale, scope, and agglomeration will all contribute to the determination of an ideal business size.

Particular industries tend to affect the size of firms. For example, manufacturers of heavy equipment with large labor and capitol demands tend to be larger than candy manufacturers, whose needs differ dramatically. Managers must constantly be attentive to their competitive positions, costs, market share, and growth potential to adequately predict the ideal size of their companies. A fluid business environment makes these decisions both crucial and difficult.

Firms that become too large may encounter problems that impair their

- 23 -

efficiency and productivity. the usual result of too large firms is an increase in cost resulting in decreased profits. Several problems are common when a business grows too quickly or reaches an unwieldy size.

Many times rapid growth causes duplication of essential production or marketing functions. Overall communication can slow, with the result that a firm may be less responsive to changes in the economy or their markets. As firms grow, a certain inertia may set in, an unwillingness to change business practices that are outmoded. Increased size almost always results in more managers who are further removed from the vital operations of the company. Sometimes a company will end up competing with itself in some areas. companies can grow so quickly they lose touch with their customers and fail to accurately assess changing markets. Rapid growth can be desirable but almost always compounds a firms problems, and often creates new ones.

As a company experiences rapid growth, the percentage of middle and upper management usually grows. Managers serve a vital function in shaping company policy, supervising operations, and planning for the future. However, managers rarely increase the productivity of a firm. Typically managers, who supervise and do not perform vital company operations, will lower the efficiency of an organization.

As firms develop over time, managers, who may be viewed as the most unproductive part of the organization, increase in numbers and influence. Sometimes managers also have dual roles as line workers who directly impact the vital operations of a firm. This is an ideal but uncommon situation. Managers who only supervise add only an intangible and incremental asset to the firm. It is not unusual to see corporations with layers of relatively unproductive middle and upper management. This almost always works to the detriment of the company.

As companies grow, it becomes more difficult to increase market share regularly. They may diversify into related industries, but at the cost of some economies of scope and scale. If a firm grows too large and too successful, it may attract negative publicity and even the attention of the government's regulatory agencies. Microsoft is an example of a firm whose dominance attracted unwelcome intervention from external sources. Wal-Mart is another successful corporation that has faced negative publicity and public scrutiny. While these are extreme examples, they occur with some frequency in the corporate world,

Larger companies tend to be those who have been in business for a long time and are set on older policies that may not apply to current business conditions. They incur additional fixed costs from pension funds, company benefits, and time lost through sickness. They often control larger portions of the market making percentage growth more difficult each year. Labor costs may include meeting union demands, and the possibility of strikes or work stoppages.

Outsized company solutions

Breaking a large unwieldy company into smaller more responsive units is often an excellent solution to overgrowth of a company. Firms will sometimes assess their operating divisions and decide to retain only the most profitable ones. Others will be sold or eliminated. Failure of a company that declares bankruptcy sometimes forces such action. Hostile takeovers of a business will almost always result in the elimination of unprofitable centers, and the reorganization of the entire company.

Government intervention is sometimes the catalyst for the reorganization of a firm that has become too monopolistic. All of these solutions are undesirable when forced upon a company from an outside source. The thoughtful and resourceful firm will take a proactive position in solving growth problems. It is much better for a company to position themselves to take advantage of growth rather than have changes imposed upon them.

Costs and revenues

Costs and revenues are the two determinants of income, the most common measuring tools for assessing business success. Firms incur fixed costs, which are constant and do not depend on that amount of production. examples would be physical plants and heavy equipment which must be paid for even if production is zero. Variable costs are tied directly to the production of finished goods and services. As more goods are produced, variable costs rise. Examples of variable costs are raw materials used in the production process, extra labor needed in peak production periods, and additional capitol if expansion is needed.

Revenue is the aggregate amount of income that the firm receives from any source. The most common source of income is the sale of deeds and services, but additional monies may be gleaned from transfer payments, investment return, and additional investment by owners. Corporations have the ability to raise money through issuing additional stock or floating bonds at attractive interest rates, as well as using venture capital to increase revenue.

Profit maximization

The usual goal of any business concern is the maximization of profits. Sole business owners, partnerships and corporations all face this problem. There are a number of common strategies for increasing profits for these concerns. The most important, for any type of business is to find the amount of production of finished goods at a certain price which guarantees the best return. One approach is to cut costs to a level to produce an optimum profit. This involves determining at what point the minimum input will result in an optimal level of per unit products. This would be a level of profit maximization.

Another tactic is to increase sales in an attempt to improve the profit picture. A flaw in this approach is that as units produced increase, variable costs also go up.

Profit maximization is determined by a myriad of economic factors, some beyond the control of an individual firm. Variables that can be determined by the firm can position it to take advantages of favorable economic conditions. Maximizing opportunities in any economic environment is the challenge for an individual company.

Pricing

Pricing is an essential element in marketing. It is a sophisticated business practice, and one that may cause a products success or failure. The simple definition of pricing is the assignment of monetary amounts to goods and services sold by the company. Complexities of this process include varying prices to different customers, special price promotions, determining the price based on fluctuating variable costs, special quantity pricing, incentive pricing for multiple orders of dissimilar products, and accurately assessing the price the market will bear.

Pricing must be based on accurate market research which provides insights to the buying habits of the potential market. Clear objectives for pricing must be set, and knowledge of the competitions pricing policies are critical. Decisions must be made on multiple pricing, pricing for international sales, zone pricing (varying prices in different geographical areas), the use of discounts, and the understanding of the market's price sensitivity. All of those factors (and several others) will determine the price charged for a particular good or service.

Prices are determined to fulfill several purposes, the main one being a sufficient price to insure sales that will attain the financial goals of the firm. The price must also be realistic when compared to the marketplace and competition. It would be an error to price a new candy bar at $1.00 if competing bars of similar size sell for $.75. Price must also fit into a company's overall marketing plan which will include channels of distribution, manufacturing requirements, and storing and shipping facilities.

The quality of the product in the market (high-end/low-end), planned promotional and overall marketing strategies, and the effectiveness of the sales force all play a part in pricing. In general prices should reflect the most that customers are willing to pay for it. This will usually result in the most income per unit. The effective price of a product is monies the firm obtains from sales of goods and services after special pricing strategies (promotions, incentives, and discounts) are considered.

There are several special pricing strategies used in different phases of the life of the product.

When a product is introduced, an introductory lower price may induce people to try the product. The goal is to secure a market base and then raise the price to a more appropriate level.

Sometimes a price is applied that is near the highest part of the pricing scale. This is intended to underscore the quality of the product and is sometimes called premium pricing. Retailers sometimes use artificially lower prices on some products to attract customers in the hope they will make additional purchases. This is called "loss leader" pricing. Demand pricing is any pricing tactic that is based on market research into consumer demand for the product.

Consumers tend to believe a higher price (within reason) relates to a higher quality product. Products may be sold together (bundled) at a special price. Economies of scope, scale, and agglomeration all play an important role in special pricing strategies.

Suggested retail price and MSRP

Manufacturers will often make a recommendation as to the retail price of a product. This is usually an effort to insure that the product is sold at a similar price in various locations. Retailers take different approaches to these suggested prices. Some will adhere to the suggested price, while others will discount the price and feature the reduced price as a promotion. Retailers may use their size and/or market position to price goods significantly cheaper than more poorly positioned retailers.

An example of this is the price comparisons on almost all unregulated goods between discount houses, convenience stores, and normal retail outlets. Often prices are set based on the wholesale prices charged to the retailers by suppliers.

Fair trade laws were enacted to protect small retailers from unfair competition from discount houses and chain retail operations. These laws were deemed to be illegal as they restrained free trade.

Manufacturers responded with the "Manufacturer's Suggested Retail Price" (MSRP), which only provides guidelines for retailers. Usually the MSRP is heavily discounted in order to suggest a product is an excellent bargain at that price.

Competition

Each state has enacted laws designed to control competition practices of businesses. These laws cover many aspects of competition, but are generally designed to insure competition is not impeded. They protect small businesses and consumers against the possible abuses of oligopolies and monopolies.

Each nation which encourages free trade has its own laws to protect competition. However the adequacy of these laws and the stringency with which they are enforced vary widely among countries of the world.

Perhaps the United States is most vigilant in these areas, having scores of anti-trust laws on the books to protect competition. In America, the Department of Justice monitors all proposed mergers and acquisitions to insure they will not significantly reduce competition. They have the power to deny such mergers and takeovers if they feel the public interest is negatively affected. The government has the ability to force large monopolistic conglomerates to break up if they unfairly control markets.

There is no such thing as perfect competition in the real world. It exists only as an economic model, describing a theoretical market where the base of producers and consumers is so large that they are unable to influence prices. Ideally this would lead to a textbook definition of economic efficiency. For perfect competition to exist, products are essentially the same, each type being an equal substitute for another. Prices are set by the market, and firms must accept this determination. All businesses must have equal access to existing information, raw materials, and the latest technology.

Monopolistic competition has a different set of standards. Usually there are numerous producers and a great number of consumers in any market. No regulations exist to entering or leaving the market, and consumers have more product knowledge and have definite choices between products. These markets give individual companies more influence over their markets. They may raise or lower prices and make adjustments based on the response of the market.

When any particular market is controlled by a small group of suppliers an oligopoly is said to exist. In this situation all suppliers are cognizant of each other's activities. When any one firm makes an economic decision, it will impact the activity of all other firms in the oligopoly. There is a great deal of interaction between members of oligopolies, and planning by any one firm must consider the likely responses of all other members. Oligopolies were very common in certain industries but anti-trust laws have limited their power.

In an oligopsony market there are limited numbers of buyers and an unlimited number of sellers. When a relative few number of businesses are in competition to acquire factors of production this situation is common. Here buyers will have a competitive advantage and will be aware of each other's economic activity.

Sometimes a situation arises where there are only a few buyers and a few sellers. this unusual situation results in a bilateral oligopsony.

When one supplier is the sole seller of a service or product a monopoly is said to exist. There is no competition in a monopolistic economy as there is only one provider or seller. Usually in a monopoly there are no ready substitutes for the products being supplied. Some monopolies are legal in a sense, a prime example being AT&T before it was broken up by government intervention. Legal monopolies are common in government agencies and institutions, and sometimes exist in specialized private sectors of the economy.

Sometimes an economic phenomena occurs where there is only a single consumer of a product, and there may be a number of suppliers. This is called monopsony, and only occurs in specialized industries that have large institutional consumers.

Cartels differ from monopolies by coordinating the action of a few suppliers to gain economic advantage. Cartels are several firms acting in concert to create an economic advantage. Cartels organize and act as if one business in order to control a finite market.

When an industry or portion of a industry is so dominated by a company that it controls the market completely a "de facto monopoly" is said to exist. This condition is sometimes called monopolistic competition. The dominance of the Microsoft company in computer software in the 1980's and 90's created monopolistic competition. Government intervention has interceded in this situation in the last few years.

Sometimes a large corporation will buy or control smaller firms who are considered competitors, and create a horizontal monopoly. These companies may have different names and trademarks but still belong to the parent corporation. This type of economic organization is called a horizontal monopoly.

A vertical monopoly is the control of associated goods and services by one corporation. For example, an oil company may own oil fields, refineries, and distribution channels to retailers in order to control an entire production and marketing flow for a product.

To qualify as a monopoly several conditions must exist. Primarily, there is only one producer or supplier of a good or service and attempts for other firms to enter as competitors are discouraged by economic action of the monopoly holder. This action may be based on better or unique technology, patents on products that allow no competition, and the economic realities of trying to enter a market that is controlled by such a dominating economic entity. These actions and others like them are collectively called blocking the entry to a monopolistic market. These economic actions may or may not be in restraint of trade.

In a monopolistic situation the product being monopolized usually has no comparable substitutes or alternatives. It can have no true competition forcing consumers to buy from the monopolizing corporation. The company controlling the monopoly can manipulate the price and available supply of the product involved. Artificial shortages can be created that force prices upward.

Business organizations

Business organizations operate under a bevy of laws and regulations that mandate both their organization and activities. There are a number of types of organization that companies may choose. The most common form of business entity is the sole proprietorship. An example of this would be "mom and pop" businesses found everywhere. Partnerships bring together two or more individuals as joint owners of a business. There are a number of various types of partnerships that define, limit, and regulate business practices and liabilities. Most familiar is the corporate form of business organization. Many familiar United States companies are organized and run as corporations.

Besides these more common forms of organization, specialized types of arrangements such as limited liability companies, cooperatives formed by individuals for specific economic purposes, government owned institutions, and pension funds and credit unions may be found in most economies.

A privately owned business with one principle owner who operates in his or her own name is called a sole proprietorship. Such an organization essentially functions as an individual who incurs any debts or liabilities of the business as personal obligations. For example, a law suit against a sole proprietorship that gains a judgment could seek compensation from both the business and the individual.

Taxation affects the sole proprietorship much like an individual, in that he or she is taxed on personal and business income. Requirements for accounting and regulations are much simpler for the sole proprietorship type of organization. Individuals owning small businesses may still choose to name their business as they wish and can file for a registered trade name that allows them to do business under that name rather than their own. Even in these cases the individual remains responsible for the debts and liabilities of his or her business.

Partnerships are business organizations where two or more individuals enter into an agreement to share in the financial proceeds,(or losses) of a business in which they have invested resources. General partners are fully responsible for

all liabilities the partnership incurs to third parties. Limited partners, while still liable for debts and obligations of the partnership, have their exposure limited to the extent they are invested in the organization. Silent partners are those who take no active role in operating the business, and may or may not be publicly associated with the firm.

Partnerships often involve legal formality of declaring their intention to do business. An formal agreement of partnership may be prepared, a public announcement made of the formation of the partnership, and some jurisdictions require partnerships to register and make available their records to the public. These usually include only the terms of the partnership and not financial records.

Generally a limited partnership operates under the same conditions as a general partnership with the exception that one or more limited partners join one or more general partners in the organization. General partners have all the rights and liabilities of any business owner. Limited partners initially make a specific investment of funds to the partnership, and their liability for debts and judgments against the partnership is limited to the amount of their investment. Limited partners have no role in managing the operations of the partnership, except in an advisory capacity. They are however required to publically declare their ownership by various registration procedures.

Organizations of professionals, such as physicians, attorneys, and other such groups often form Limited Liability Partnerships which places various limits on the financial exposure of each partner. Limits and statutes vary between states, but often partners are protected from liability in a judgment simply because they belong to the organization.

Corporations

The term "corporation" is a legal one, defining the rules and regulations for a business, non-profit organization, or institution to incorporate. Governmental entities such as cities and towns may also choose to incorporate. Voluntary associations need not apply for corporate status.

Corporations often operate as an individual person might, with power to make agreements, own land and capital equipment, and participate in business. In a sense, a corporation is a person under the law, and subject to rules and regulations any person must abide by. Additionally, there are specific obligations a corporation must perform, including public registration, and other regulations deemed necessary by the state in which the corporation intends to do business. Corporations differ from individuals in some important ways. They cannot cast votes in public elections, nor cab they, as an entity be imprisoned (although individual members of the corporation could be incarcerated).

Corporations must file formal documents with a state describing the particulars of the intended corporation. This includes any stock issues (public or private)the identity of officers of the proposed corporation, and the general rules and operating procedures for the corporation. The laws of the state in which the corporation in licensed regulate its business practices, including many financial restrictions.

When stock is issued, share holders of a corporation may be individuals, institutions, other corporations or government agencies. If no stock is involved in the corporation, it may still incorporate and often is called a "society," "membership corporation," or another title indicating no stock is outstanding for the corporation.

There is usually a board of officers and directors who operate the corporation on behalf of the owners. This board is responsible for the financial affairs of the company, as well as making policy and human resource decisions, including the appointment or election of the major officers of the firm.

When the term corporation is used to describe a business organization, what immediately comes to mind is a business that issues common or preferred stock that is publicly traded on an organized stock exchange. More accurately, this type of business organization is called a public corporation. Many large and familiar firms fall into this category.

Privately held or closed corporations are much more common. These entities may issue stock to a select number of officers, but there is no public trading on any organized market. Both individuals and companies may be the stockholders of these "closed corporations." They usually include only a relatively small number of stockholders.

Some corporations have expanded (or were originally organized) to do business all over the world. The phenomena of globalization has witnessed the increasing number and economic power of what we now term "multinational corporations."

These companies are regulated in each country in which they do business. Some are separately incorporated in multiple countries.

Welfare economics

The common economic good of society is the domain of welfare economics. It is concerned with the distribution of resources and income throughout an economy. Although welfare economics is a macroeconomic field, it uses microeconomic observation and analysis to formulate theory and policy. The aggregate economic activity of all individuals is studied to gauge the impact on the total society.

Taking the individual as the economic unit to be studied, welfare economics does not concern itself with economic behavior of different sectors of the economy. The individual is studied as the unit that understands and promotes its own welfare, whether that welfare is measured in money, assets, or other economic considerations. One could say welfare economics addresses the overall satisfaction and welfare of the society, regardless of what economic system is in operation. The welfare of all individuals equals the welfare of the society.

Parento efficiency

An important economic theory that studies the effects of alternative choices in resource allocation is Parento Efficiency. This is an important analytic tool in modern economics. First posited by the Italian economist Vilfredo Parento, it seeks to study the level of economic efficiency determined by the distribution of income.

Simply stated, if a change in the allocation of resources improves the economic condition of one individual or group, without hurting another individual or group, this is called Parento improvement. Parento efficiency is a sophisticated economic analytical tool that incorporates aspects of mathematics, social science, and engineering. If an economy is proved to be Parento efficient, then no individual or group within that economy can be improved by switching allocations of resources without degrading the economic condition of

another individual or group in that economy.

In this case, no shift of resources will benefit the society.

Social Welfare Function

An economic tool which measures the economic welfare of a given society, after considering all relevant economic factors, is called the Social Welfare Function. There are a number of possible standards for measuring the social welfare of an economy, including financial, social, and political elements.

First introduced by the economist Abram Bergson in the 1930's, social welfare was posited to be the aggregate level of want satisfying attainment by all individuals in a society. In some sense, social welfare reflects the values and goals of a society. In the United States for example, a social and economic goal is to make retired and older citizens who cannot work economically better off. To achieve this social and economic objective, the government has introduced transfer payment programs over the years primarily through social security. Another objective is to provide those unable to work with sufficient income to be economically viable. Unemployment and disability transfer payments by state and federal governments seeks to attain this.

Income inequality distribution measurement

The measurement of income distribution in an economy is done by a set of analytical tools collectively called Income Distribution Metrics. The overall purpose of this analysis is to identify patterns of wealth in a society and determine the fairness or inequality of the economy.

One set of techniques sets a standard for income and then determines the number of individuals who fall below that line. This approach is most effective in measuring the degree of poverty in a given economy. Examples of these tools in the United States include the poverty line and the number of people living below it.

Another group of tools compares income levels between groups and individuals in order to determine how income is distributed in a society and locate patterns of inequality. There are a number of these type of analytical techniques with the relative poverty line and the Lorenz Curve being the best known.

The Lorenz Curve

One of the most useful indicators of equality and inequality in income distribution in an economy is the Lorenz Curve. Developed in the early 20th century by Max Lorenz, it paints a graphical representation of the distribution of income in a society. The Lorenz curve first posits a state of perfect income equality, and compares actual income distribution with the ideal. Another use of the Lorenz Curve is to plot the patterns of asset distribution in an economy.

The Lorenz Curve can indicate what percentage of total income certain economic individuals or household hold. This is done by creating a graph of the curve with each point measuring relative income. For example we may learn that 70% of the total income of an economy is held by 30% of the households. The Lorenz curve provides a schedule that charts these ratios.

The Lorenz curve and other such relative indicators of income distribution are sometimes used in welfare economics to measure the equality of the economic system. Many social programs are based on these analyses.

Poverty line

The term "poverty line" is one that is commonly used in assessing the success or failure of an economic system. A level of income that fails to reach the minimum for people to purchase the necessities of life is the poverty line. Individuals or households falling below this line are unable to provide for themselves, and have zero disposable income.

Of course, a key consideration is where to draw the poverty line on the economic scale. Because of different prices and costs of living, and varied wage scales, poverty lines are different for each country. When comparing poverty lines between countries, the accepted standard is the purchasing power exchange rate. This reveals the relative ability between countries to buy, say, a loaf of bread.

Poverty exists to some degree in almost all economic systems. The line is an excellent tool to measure the number and percent of those living in poverty and may form the basis of remedial social programs.

How should poverty lines be determined is a question each economy faces as it develops social and economic policy. Some countries use a fixed figure and adjust it for inflation and deflation. The criteria used to determine the fixed figure can vary between countries to a large degree.

Comparing poverty lines among countries is a complex and sometimes frustrating problem, as prices, wages, and standards fluctuate over time. For example, the European Common Market first computes the median household income and arbitrarily sets the poverty line at 60% of that figure. In the United States, the poverty line is based on a Social Security system that makes certain arbitrary levels of income as poverty levels. the government then uses transfer payments to insure a minimum income to all households based on a tangle of federal, state, and local regulations. While this is admirable from a social point of view it remains vague and arbitrary from an economic perspective.

Absolute poverty

Absolute levels of poverty exist only in economic theory. It is not economically possible to project a universal poverty line for all individuals in the world. This imaginary poverty line cannot fluctuate even if income distribution changes. The theoretical basis for this universal poverty line is that there is a minimum amount of goods necessary to survive and that that amount does not vary worldwide. To accurately compute such a figure the total of all consumption must be known and accounted for. This is not possible from a practical point-of-view. Absolute poverty will decline when everyone's income in an economy rises, even if the distribution of wealth does not change. An absolute poverty rate may decline regardless of whether inequality is remedied as long as the neediest obtain some increase in income. From this brief analysis it can be seen that an absolute poverty line is meaningless in and of itself. Unless a comparison of income levels within the same economy is measured, there is never a guarantee of accurate and meaningful poverty lines.

Relative poverty

Only when a poverty line is fixed in relationship to other economic information does it have validity in the real world. A poverty line must be relative to some other economic indicator. For example, median income may be a relative standard with which to measure poverty. One could then define poverty as a certain percentage of income below the median income. In such a case the general increase in income in a society may increase, but the poverty line will remain the same.

Poverty equals inequality is a general sense. An evening of income distribution will cause relative poverty to fall. Welfare economists sometimes prefer the term inequality to relative poverty. The subjective nature of defining poverty is apparent. For example a level of income that more than takes care of necessities may still be relatively low for the economy as a whole. The arbitrary assignment of a poverty level relative to other economic measurements is by definition subjective.

Externality

When an economic decision made by a person who has no economic gain or loss at stake results in a significant impact on others it is said to be an externality. This occurs when the decision maker is in a neutral position regarding any gains and losses from the decision. The catalyst for the decision makes economic choices that affect others with no risk. Governments often make such decisions that have an important impact on others but not to the individual who makes the choice. Examples of externalities would be the permission to drill for oil on a nature preserve. The decision may be made in Washington by a government official who has no financial interest in petroleum and does not live near the natural habitat. Yet the decision will have far reaching effects on a large group of suppliers and consumers.

Externalities may usually be traced back to a demand and supply situation. An increase need for oil may have determined the decision for oil exploration in a natural habitat.

Social costs

Every economic decision has a social cost closely linked to it. The technical definition of the social costs of an economic action is the aggregate cost of that activity to society as a whole, as well as any costs incurred by the unit or agency making the decision.

Negative externality is a situation that takes place when the social cost to society is greater than the cost to the decision maker. The classic example of negative externality is manufacturing pollution. This has a huge social (and economic) cost that is seldom paid for directly by the firm causing the pollution. When the costs are greater to the private sector than to society, a positive externality is in effect.

Social costs are a major topic and economic measurement in welfare economics. Activists measure social costs and employ them in their arguments for social, political, and economic policy.

Free goods

In economic analysis, a free good is used rather loosely to designate a good or service that is abundant. This means such goods are available to everyone at little or no cost to the economy. Examples of free goods include natural resources owned by the public, water, and air. Some free goods are so easily available in , that everyone can have as much as they want under ordinary circumstances.

Other free goods may be the result of cooperation between economic entities, including governments to yield an excess of a good for the general welfare. Some free goods are intangible. Examples would include the skies used by airlines, the oceans used to fish and dredge for assets, and ideas or inventions that fall into the public domain. A modern economic intangible is the creation on internet technology which is a complex combination of ideas, cutting edge technology, and public access. No one owns the internet, yet is used for a myriad number of economic (and personal) purposes.

Taxation

Any assessment or charge to an individual economic unit by a government or quasi-government may be termed a tax. Some taxes are direct, such as a sales tax on goods and services sold. Other taxes may be indirect, property taxes being a prime example.

Taxation has a long history dating back to biblical times. It is often mentioned in the Old and New Testaments. Earlier economic systems received "taxes" as goods and services rendered to a ruling authority. In contemporary economics, we usually think of taxes in terms of legal currency.

Taxes have caused revolutions, "No taxation without representation," overturned governments, and have become a social and political issue of controversy and debate. Who should pay taxes, how much should be paid, and the use of tax revenue are all critical issues in the fabric of society. The branch of formal economics most concerned with taxes is public finance.

Nations, states, and local governments use taxes to finance their operations and for special purposes. Typical uses of tax revenue are for public utilities, promotion of public safety and defense, reinvesting in capital improvement and replacement projects for the public, general operating expenses of the state, and to fund public and welfare services.

Other uses for tax revenues include social benefits for retired and disabled citizens, public transportation systems, compensation for those unable to work, educational uses, public health and healthcare systems, and waste removal operations.

Governments also use taxes to stimulate or contract the economy, alter resource allocations in the economic system, insure an equitable tax burden on all citizens, and to change patterns of income distribution for members of a society. Taxation and its revenues have become an important proactive tool for economists attempting to fine tune macroeconomic activities.

Tax rates

Tax rates are a percentage figure levied on the tax base to raise revenues. When the tax base is a good, service, or property, the tax is called an ad valorem tax. Examples of ad valorem taxes are common, including most property and sales taxes. Value added taxes, common in Western Europe, add a "hidden" tax to all goods and services, (with a few exceptions) computed on the added value at each stage of the manufacturing process. Excise taxes is a tax levied on a tax base of a determined figure. Excess profit taxes are an example of an excise tax.

Tax rates may be either marginal rates or average rates. To compute the average tax rate, the total tax revenue is compared to the total tax base as a ratio. Marginal tax rates are those imposed on the next unit of currency earned. For example, in a progressive income taxation system the marginal tax rate will differ from person to person, depending on their income. Typically tax brackets are the framework for determining marginal rates of taxes at various income levels.

Types of taxation

A "flat tax" is one in which the same tax rate applies to all levels of income. For example, a country may have an income tax of 40% on every taxpayer's income, regardless of the level. Someone earning $10,000 a year would pay 40% of that figure. Another individual earning $100,000 a year would pay the same tax rate, 40%, but the dollar amount would differ dramatically.

Regressive tax systems have a reduced schedule of tax rates as income rises. Thus someone making $10,000 a year would pay a higher tax rate than someone making $100,000 a year. Progressive income tax systems, as we employ in the United States, tax higher levels of income more than lower levels. Progressive tax systems are thought to be the most fair as they place the largest tax burden on those with the most income.

People are seldom happy with any system of taxation and the entire issue has become a political one with almost all people calling for tax reform of one type or another.

Direct taxes are defined as those that are imposed and collected directly from the economic units being taxed. For example, income taxes are levied and collected from the individual or business that actually receives monies as income. Indirect taxes, by contrast, are collected from a third party who is not the being actually taxed. Value added taxes are indirect taxes, hidden from the consumer who pays an increased retail or wholesale price that includes the value added tax.

Statutes determine for whom the tax is being collected. The individual who ends up paying the tax is another matter. For example, a tax may be placed on alcoholic beverages of all kinds. Only those who choose to consume these products will actually be subject to the tax. Laws of supply and demand in the marketplace will determine the individuals that will pay this tax. if an individual chooses not to buy wine, beer, or liquor, they will be, in effect, exempt from that tax. the more a person consumes the taxed items, the more tax will be paid by that individual.

Most income tax systems in modern economies are progressive in that they increase the tax rate as income rises. Progressive tax systems are favored by those who feel the brunt of taxation should be on those who can more easily afford it. Conservative economists (and politicians) argue that this form of taxation is punishing the economically successful and is a deterrent to economic growth. The nature of tax collection and the private information required to administer the system angers some who feel the government is increasingly intrusive in their lives.

The nature of tax collection was revolutionized by the concept of withholding taxes directly from an individual's paycheck. This serves to aid tax compliance as the taxes are automatically collected each pay period. Psychologically, it seems less burdensome to the taxpayer who never actually has the money. People have come to accept their salaries as being "take home pay", the actual disposable income available to them after taxes are withheld. Capital gains taxes may be levied whenever a major capital asset is sold. Capital gains taxes may be applied as a regular tax when the capital gain is called income. In certain circumstances, special tax rates are applicable to capital gains and a part of the gain is exempt from taxation. Corporations and affluent individuals are the beneficiaries of capital gains tax schedules. Tax rules, statutes, and the tax codes provide a number of tax shelters for corporations. Tax "loopholes" are exploited by corporate tax attorneys

and accountants to minimize the tax burden of corporations.

Income earned by corporations also may benefit from special tax rates. Depreciation of major assets and deductions for major assets provide favorable tax breaks for corporations. Corporations may exempt or defer taxes from income flow by using these special considerations. Corporate taxes are often the targets of criticism from social and economic activists who feel they are granted special privileges not available to individuals.

Real estate is subject to taxation in the form of a property tax. Property taxes may also be levied by governments for personal property such as automobiles. The usual method of determining a property tax is to assess the value of the property on a regular basis, and apply the existing tax rate to this base. Property taxes are a prime method of financing education in the United States.

Taxes on estates and on inheritances have both their advocates and critics. Some believe large estates should be taxed as they are most able to pay. Others argue this discriminates against the wealthy and economically successful individual. As mentioned above, personal property taxes may be levied on many kinds of assets, including autos and boats to name only a couple. Critics argue there is no rationale for these taxes and they simply serve to fill government coffers. Auto registration and license fee at least offer a privilege (driving) for their levy.

Tragedy of the commons

In the constant competition for resources between components of an economy there arises a phenomena called "the tragedy of the commons." This controversy begs the question as to the ownership on natural resources such as the seas and atmosphere. Can individuals claim as their own the vast resources of the planet or do they belong to all? Should these resources be used for individual gain or to promote the general welfare? These are the questions raised by the tragedy of the commons, a term coined by Garrett Hardin.

The concept has been expanded in contemporary economics to describe perceived selfish behavior in all living things. The drive for survival and dominance in nature as well as economics provides ample examples of the primacy of self interest. From this self interest and its results, the common good often suffers because of individual actions. This is the larger meaning of the tragedy of the commons.

Contemporary examples of the tragedy of the commons are evident in all aspects of society. Pollution in all its forms, including air pollution and water pollution are prime examples of the tragedy of the commons. The irresponsible consumption of logging in forests, depletion of ocean's resources by over harvesting and pollution, the indiscriminate littering and graffiti common in cities, and traffic congestion causing additional pollution and lowered quality of life are all part of the tragedy of the commons.

Less obvious but still destructive are noise pollution, legalized gambling, the seamier sides of the internet, including pornography and massive spamming, all have negative impacts on the quality of life because of the selfish action of special groups and interests. Whenever there is a degrading of the general welfare in any manner by a small percentage of the population the tragedy of the commons is seen.

Tragedy of the anticommons

When there is a collective or individual activity that results in an under-use of a scarce resource this is the tragedy of the anticommons. Contrasted with the tragedy of the commons, which is an overuse or misuse of a scarce resource, which negatively affects the general welfare. If a resource is ignored or under-utilized by large numbers of individuals, a different type of waste occurs. This situation is common when a large segment of the economic society is excluded by some means from access to the resource. Common contemporary examples are found in bio-medical and pharmacological research , where patents prevent cooperative development of therapeutic drugs and technology. Property rights are often cited as an example of tragedy of the anticommons as they exclude a large number of individuals from fully participating in the economic system. When a large part of society is denied access to a fundamental economic activity, that activity may be said to be under-used because the resource is available only to a relative few.

Efficient market theory

The mechanisms and activity of capital markets is explained by efficient market theory. Using the price of an equity as an example, the price of a stock or bond is a result of all known information and news about the equity and market. This total information results in a rational estimation of the true intrinsic value of the equity. Such a price will have accounted for all positive and negative information of the equity. The price may be said to be discounted, or adjusted for all known information. Should anyone have special access to such information, they are in a position of competitive advantage relative to the equity.

This theory makes certain assumptions about the market. These include a large market with many individuals trading for the equity, the presence of perfect information about the stock and market, and free and equal access to all information. Market news is assumed to rise randomly and be available to all at the same time. Efficient market theory is rarely seen in the real world, because the necessary conditions for such a condition to exist almost never occur.

Financial economics

The branch of economics which deals with business finance, including financing individual firms and corporations is called financial economics. This field also encompasses the financial markets, commodity exchanges, and money markets. Financial economics is governed by several basic principles: Risk or uncertainty - the gain or loss of monetary assets is not presently known, but will be determined in the future by economic determinants. The element of time - the monetary gain or loss changes over time. Economic options - any party to an economic exchange is free to make a decision that will affect future results. Economic information - economic information can alter future economic activity, result in monetary gains and losses, and change the dynamics of the participants.

Financial economics considers the determinants of prices of financial assets, alternatives for business financing, and personal business decisions that result in reaching economic objectives.

Time value of money

A basic precept of business finance is the time value of money. Known also as the discounted present value of money, this principle is crucial in decision making in business finance. Stated simply, the time value of money means an individual would rather have his or her money now,

than in the future. If the possession of the money is deferred, a price is paid for the delay. This price reflects the time value of money. For example, if $10 today will accrue to $12 in one year, the time value of money for that period is $2.

The time value of money concerns itself with future risk. The value of money today might be worth more or less in the future, depending on inflation or deflation. An investor or lender (or borrower) gives up a certain value today for an uncertain value sometime in the future. The astute individual will evaluate economic conditions with a view toward predicting the future value of money and base his or her economic decisions on that projection.

Study of finance

The use of money as an economic resource includes the individual and business decisions regarding the obtaining, utilization, and allocation of financial resources after evaluating risk potential. Thus finance studies the uses of money and comparable assets, and the effective management of these assets, risk appraisal and the provision of funds for business operations. Finance is also defined as the collective policies and operations that business entities (or individuals) manage their business activities with. Primary aspects of these operations include management of income and costs, and alternatives in investment choices.

These choices are determined by management decisions as how best to utilize excess income. Excess income may be invested, loaned to borrowers, or reinvested in the business to improve operations. These economic decisions are important to the growth and economic health of the entity.

Business finance

Corporate or managerial finance is the process of acquiring and using funds for business operations. This requires an assessment of potential risk and opportunity for the utilization of monies. Decisions regarding the capital structure of a firm, either by equity financing or the issuing of bonds, must be made. The monies necessary for operations, or working capital, may be provided by income from operations or by a line of credit from a lending institution.

Firms may choose to issue bonds to finance operations. The company sells the bonds which carry an interest rate, to investors. These bonds may be traded on the open market, and the price will fluctuate with interest rates. Financial managers of companies may choose to use profits to invest in an array of possible investments, each positioned for a different strategy. The financial function of businesses is critical for their success, both in the short term and over a long period. Strategies vary according to the overall position of the firm, their industry goals, and the financial health of the firm.

Risk

Risk is the possible negative effect a business activity or decision carries. Risk assessment includes both the probability of a negative event and the assessment of the impact of the potential event. Risk varies from industry to industry, and can be applied to a variety of business (or individual) decisions. Risks are an inevitable part of business, and the object of a firm is to minimize risk and maximize return.

Business risks include marketing decisions, financial choices, production and product delivery systems, and a myriad of other business functions. Financial risks are considered to be

excellent testing grounds for other business decisions. Current thinking in risk appraisal involves predicting the level of exposure and vulnerability if the potential risk is realized. Managers ask themselves what results they would be willing to live with should the risk become an event. This assessment includes a multitude of factors that must be considered depending on the nature and possible impact of the risk in question.

International trade and tariffs

Tariffs are in effect, a tax on goods imported from other countries. Goods cannot be delivered and sold before a tariff is paid. Tariffs have broad implications in international trade and consequently in relations between nations. Tariffs may be calculated by the weight of goods, or as a percentage of the value of the item. The latter case is termed an ad valorem tax. Sometimes governments impose tariffs as a purely money making function, and these are termed revenue tariffs.

Tariffs are widely used by countries to protect their own exports and to defend their own industries from competition from abroad. Tariffs add to the price of imported goods, affording a price advantage to local products. A protective tariff can be so high as to be prohibitive, so that no imports are economically viable. Tariffs have become both political and economic weapons for competing nations. Tariffs have historically been opposed by "free traders," who believe unfettered trade is the healthiest economic environment and works to the benefit of all countries involved.

General equilibrium theory

General equilibrium theory provides a picture of the entire economy beginning with individuals and their markets. An important part of microeconomics, it models an infinite number of markets for goods and services beginning with the most basic units in the economy. In this manner, it portrays the entire economy as a sum of all its individual units. It differs from macroeconomics, which begins its analysis of the economy using aggregate numbers. Modern general equilibrium theory is a highly sophisticated tool and requires the use of computer technology to generate its models. The vast numbers of individuals and markets included in such an analysis would not have been possible until the widespread use of computers in economic analysis. Generating economic aggregates from individual transactions allows economists to build a model of the economy with a degree of accuracy. It answers the question of how macroeconomics obtains its data.

A relatively new tool of economists, the general equilibrium theory promises both comprehensive and accurate raw material with which to build a model of the entire economy.

Heteroeconomics

Any school of economic theory which differs substantially from modern neoclassical economic theory is classified as heteroeconomics. The main argument of heteroeconomics is that most contemporary economic thinking tend to focus on the results of economic activity rather than the dynamics of that activity. Rather than posit what may happen when specific conditions of supply, demand, consumption, and pricing exist, heteroeconomics looks at the interaction between economic elements in a society. This more comprehensive view allows for a more sophisticated understanding of how economies work and the way in which each component affects others. Their are a number of schools of heteroeconomics and all of them use a

broader framework than neoclassical analysis. Drawing from all the social sciences as well as other fields, heteroeconomics is a sometimes a more "real world" view of economic activity and interaction. Neoclassical economists consider heteroeconomics a very inexact science and are critical of the ambitious scope of most heteroeconomic thought.

Heterodox economics refers to schools of economic thought which do not conform to the mainstream paradigm of neoclassical economics. Examples of heteroeconomics include bioeconomics, evolutionary economics and complexity economics to name only a few.

Evolutionary economics

Evolutionary economics is a new and growing field in heteroeconomics. Modeled on the life sciences, it looks at economic activity as complex, dynamic, interactions with elements of scarcity, growth, and the striving for competitive advantages. In a sense, evolutionary economics imposes Darwin's theory of evolution on economic conditions to explain both behavior and results. Survival of the fittest may be applied to business concerns, with the most adaptable succeeding and those unable to select economic survival capabilities failing and forced to suspend operations. Firms must survive by combining a product mix appropriate for their markets with effective business practices. As conditions change, those businesses that are able to maintain flexibility and measured responses to a changing economic environment will survive, while less responsive firms will fall away. Companies that succeed tend to continue innovative practices that allow them to achieve success. Those who fail to respond to economic change will not survive in the long run.

Neoclassical economics

Neoclassical economics is founded on certain assumptions about economic activities. Based on the theories of supply and demand, it assumes rational decisions being made by all economic units. Each unit will attempt to maximize their gain or individual economic satisfaction through these decisions, which are based on the economic information available to them. Neoclassical economics is to a large degree what we call mainstream economic theory. Critics of neoclassical economics have been effective in showing obvious flaws in many of the assumptions of the school. These criticisms have often evolved into new schools of economic thought seeking to find a more realistic way of understanding economic decisions and their results. The very definition of what constitutes neoclassical economics is an area of debate, as neoclassical economists have a wide variety of approaches and analyses for most economic problems. The areas of disagreement from within neoclassical economics and from those who challenge the basic premises of the field have caused a degree of confusion in economic study. It is safe to say that neoclassical economics is in a state of relative flux as new and revised thinking is brought to economic analysis.

Austrian school of economics

The 20th century saw the birth of the Austrian school of economics, a hybrid school that stands outside the traditional schools of mainstream economic theory. Perhaps the most important proponent of the Austrian school is Carl Menger, who with his associates and colleagues pioneered the economic theory upon which the Austrian school was founded.

Anti-Keynesian in approach, the Austrian school has rejected the bioeconomic model of imposing the principles of life sciences to the subject of economics. Employing a logical and intuitive set of tools collectively called praxeology, the Austrian school takes a more formal approach to economic theory. The success of the Austrian school has been influential by focusing on the generative stage of economic productivity. It has successfully challenged for many the behavioral basis of economic theory, in favor of more traditional formal aspects of cause and effect in economic theory. Groups or political associations that profess a libertarian or liberal philosophy view the Austrian school favorably and share many of their social and political goals.

Behavioral economics

Behavioral economics draws heavily from a number of social sciences and related fields to attempt to understand the behaviors and emotional components of economic activities. Working with the traditional economic framework of allocation of scarce resources, supply, demand, and pricing policy, behavioral economics inquires in to the reasoning and motivation for economic choices. They study the rational behavior of economic entities, and attempt to predict results based on these rational decisions.

Behavioral economics posits "heuristics," that decision making is often intuitive or behavioral rather than strictly rational. it believes that the way an economic choice is presented to a firm or individual, will determine its ultimate decision. Behavioral economics also tackles the phenomena of market inefficiencies, explaining why the behavior of markets often defy logical and expected outcomes.

Opponents of behavioral economics often base their arguments on the rational activities of an economy and its units. Contending that the behaviorists ignore market realities, particularly the ability of economic units to learn, modify their choices, and improve their opportunities for success. They feel these factors will move all players in the market toward rational decision making upon which neoclassical economics is built. They also claim that cognitive theories do not reflect general economic activity, but rather focus on a narrow area of decision-making. Thus decision making using a cognitive model cannot be validly imposed on economic decisions.

Behavioral economics relies upon survey and questionnaires to obtain data on economic choices. Critics feel these tools are often poorly constructed and fail to consider that revealed preferences are more accurate in predicting economic behavior than responses from surveys. Bias and subjectivity are sometimes incorporated into the research tools of behavioral economics, making them suspect.

Ecological economics

The increasing importance of ecology in the last half of the 20th century gave rise to the innovative field of ecological economics. This branch of economics concerns itself with the relationships between economics and extant ecosystems in the biosphere. It has common elements with the "green" movement and incorporates human development theory into its approach to economics.

The major goal of ecological economics is to protect and preserve resources through sustainable development of those resources. Sustainable development means that the resource in question will not be exploited and destroyed by irresponsible economic activity. Ecological economics positions itself as a subdivision of ecology, maintaining that economics is inherent in the interaction of ecosystems in the biosphere. It tends to place an increased importance on the use and misuse of natural resources which are seen to be the most important of the factors of production.

Profit

The word profit is derived from the Latin and means "to go forward or advance". In an economic sense, profit is the gain made from an economic transaction made by a business or individual. Profit may be defined in a multitude of ways, depending on the economic system and the method of accounting within that system. In investment transactions, profit is understood to be the return over time of an input of land, labor, and capital. In business concerns this is usually expressed as a rate of return for the assets utilized.

Most business concerns measure profit as the difference between revenue received and costs. Economists broaden this definition to include the return from an economic action when the opportunity costs of all other possible choices are considered. The drive for businesses to maximize profits is considered a stimulus to economic activity. It provides motivation and actual rewards for astute economic decisions.

Cost-benefit analysis

The determination of the best possible economic action in a situation is often formally or intuitively a result of a cost-benefit computation. An individual must ask what will the total costs be in any decision in relation to the total benefits which may be reasonably predicted. Analyzing several alternatives using this approach will yield the best decision given the information available. In business decisions this usually means what amount of resources must be used to gain a specified return or profit. Such

- 42 -

cost-benefit calculations are not limited to money. Subjective factors must be considered and sometimes an arbitrary monetary value placed on them. Economic decisions, particularly on the part of governments, must weigh economic, quality of life, political, and social elements into this analysis. For example, a government decision to drill for oil in a natural habitat will include economic considerations, as well as the impact of the decision on the well being of the society as a whole. Since almost all economic actions occur over time, the future costs and profits must be considered from a present-value perspective.

Agricultural economics

Agricultural economics reflects a more business-like approach to economics and is focused on the individual units active in agricultural activities. Courses in agricultural economics in colleges and universities tend to emphasize business practices as they relate to agriculture. By definition, this gives agricultural economics a micro-economic flavor.

The field of study in agricultural economics relates to the supply of farm commodities and domestic animals. Included in the broader scope of the field is the area of rural development, the economics of production for farm goods, and the business oriented areas of agribusiness management. Although a specialized field of economics, general economic principles such as risk, resource allocation, markets, competition, and international trade are all an important part of agricultural economics. Specialized topics include food safety, crop protection, farm production methods and techniques, rules and regulations governing agricultural economics, and the critical importance of the field to the well being of society.

Business competition

Competition is the driving force that is the life blood of capitalism. It tends to motivate innovations, and promotes efficient use of resources and profits. Microeconomic theory holds that competition is the most important factor in determining resource allocation.

Competition forces companies to develop new products and improve existing ones. It spurs technology, refines production capability, and thus provides consumers with an abundance of superior products and services. Competition tends to stabilize prices and insures no one major supplier can dominate an industry.

Competition may find two products competing head-to-head in direct competition. Sometimes firms develop similar products that may be used instead of existing ones, an example of substitute competition. Most competition is seen in pricing, production costs, product mixes, marketing, channels of distribution and consumer satisfaction. These elements fall under the umbrella of budget competition.

Wage determination

The value of real wages can only be accurately measured when the productivity of labor is known. Real wages rise when increased levels of technology and per capita investment in labor occurs. The totality of all firms demand for labor is called the total market demand for labor. The market supply of labor depends on the population, level of skill required, the prevalent economic condition and the effective wage-rate. When the demand and supply curves for labor intersect, the competitive equilibrium wage rate is determined. Firms will continue to hire labor until the marginal revenue product of labor, or its demand for labor, reaches the wage-rate.

Labor unions can distort the supply and demand for labor, and thus the wage determination, by increasing productivity, reducing the labor force with excessive union dues, and by bargaining with businesses and threatening strikes. All of these activities enter into the determination of wages.

Rent and interest

Land and other natural resources are limited in supply and thus scarce in economic terms. The price of using land and associated resources is called rent. Pricing rent differs from other factors of production as the total amount of land if fixed. The market demand and price of rent paid does not change the amount of land available for use.

Interest may be expressed as the price of using money over a period of time, usually expressed in a percentage ratio. Interest rates vary, often to a large degree, depending on the competitive environment, the amount of risk in the loan, the length of the loan and associated administrative costs involved with the loan. Demand for funds comes from individuals, businesses, and governments. The supply of money available for loan is the accrued aggregate savings of businesses and individuals. This supply is largely determined by the money supply available, which in turn is affected by the monetary policies of the government.

Reference material

Theory of Games and Economic Behavior - John Von Neumann and Oskar Morgenstern
> Description: a book by the mathematician John von Neumann and economist Oskar Morgenstern. It contains a mathematical theory of economic and social organization, based on a theory of games of strategy. This is now a classic work, upon which modern-day game theory is based.

Handbook of Econometrics- Griliches, Zvi and Intrigilator, M. D. (eds.)
> Description: a five-volume work that is the definitive study of econometrics.

The Handbook of Experimental Economics - Kagel, J. H. and Roth, A. E. (eds.)
> Description: The most influential experimental economics handbook.

Some of the most important new theories and concepts in microeconomics are published in academic journals such as " The Journal of Econometrics", "Journal of the American Statistical Society", and the "Journal of Monetary Economics". A number of professional business journals offer excellent material.

National Income and Price Determination

Microeconomics and Macroeconomics

While microeconomics studies the individual units of economic activity, macroeconomics takes a larger view. It is the analysis of the aggregate of all the economic actions of individuals, corporations and businesses. This expanded scope includes the issues of government policies that influence the economy. Such national goals include suppressing inflation, stimulating the economy through monetary and fiscal policy, and attaining a maximum employment level. The conduct and regulation of international trade is another area of national interest.

There are a multiple number of economic schools of thought that influence macroeconomics. Macroeconomics is an area of continuing evolution, and various tools of economic analysis are used from a variety of sources. The goal of all such schools is to provide the most current and precise economic data and analysis available. Research carried out by different patterns of economic thinking are combined to produce the most useful and accurate information.

Analytical approaches

The two broad divisions of economic analysis are Keynesians theory, developed in the 20th century by the English economist, John Maynard Keynes, and supply side economics, a current favorite of more conservative economists. Keynesian economics proposes government action to stimulate demand in an economy. Supply side economics is concerned with the policies that will encourage increased supply by manufacturers and other business organizations.

Keynes believed that aggregate demand was the key to understanding fluctuations in the economy. He argued for strong government interventions to attain these goals. Much of the New Deal economics applied during the depression of the 1930's was based on Keynes theories. The so called "supply-siders" emphasizes the role of the aggregate money supply and fiscal action (or inaction) as the crucial factors in economic growth.

Modern schools of macroeconomics

Milton Friedman, a Chicago economist is the chief proponent of Monetarism, that states that the supply of money in an economy is the major determinant of economic growth or deflation. It eschews the manipulation of aggregate demand in favor of monetary policy which controls the amount of money available in an economy.

Keynesian economics encourages the pro-active role of the government in stimulating aggregate demand to promote economic growth. An offshoot of this school is New Keynesian Economics which combines traditional Keynesian theory with microeconomic tools in order to spur demand.

The Post-Keynesian theorists incorporate much of Keynesian economics, but believe historical patterns in economics lead to more uncertainty in applying economic stimuli to promote demand. New Classical economics adds the concept of rational expectations to the Keynesian mix.

Austrian economics is a conservative school which believes the government's activity in economic policy leads to fluctuations in the business cycles.

Milton Friedman

The strongest advocate of the monetary school of macroeconomics is Milton Friedman, an American economist whose theories have become associated with minimal government intervention except in the regulation of the money supply. A Nobel Prize winner in 1976, Friedman's work has included the analysis of consumption as well as his emphasis on monetary theory and policy. Friedman has become an icon of conservative economists and politicians for his stance against government spending to spur the economy.

Friedman believes that inflation is a direct result of an increase in the money supply, and monetary policy the most effective tool in managing an economic system. His rejection of government playing a proactive role in increasing aggregate demand is controversial as it goes against the major themes of government activity of the last 70 years. He argues against many of the Keynesian interventions that have become part of contemporary economics.

John Maynard Keynes

Perhaps the most influential economist of the last 100 years was John Maynard Keynes. Born in 1883, Keynes lived his life and developed his theories in England during the first quarter of the 20th century. Although a great proponent of government intervention in managing the economy, Keynes was strongly opposed to socialism, which he felt would weaken a free economy. Keynes's major concerns were the management and control of business cycles, eliminating both depressions and inflation which he saw as destabilizing economic systems. His major thesis was that aggregate demand was the most important indicator of economic cycles, particularly the extremes of depression and run-away inflation.

Keynes summarized his theories in "The General Theory of Employment, Interest, and Money" which he wrote in the early 1930's. Keynes's ideas gained international acclaim and were the basis for the active government role in combating the depression in the 1930's. His ideas appeal to those who believe the responsibility of the government is to act strongly to encourage economic growth.

Robert Lucas

Robert E Lucas is regarded as one of the most important contemporary economists. A professor of Economics at the University of Chicago, Lucas was instrumental in applying microeconomic analytical methods to study the economy as a whole. His work on the theory of "Rational Expectations" was groundbreaking and added greatly to his reputation as a leading economist. He was awarded the Nobel Prize for this work in 1995.

The "Lucas Technique" investigates the dynamic relationships in an economy. It analyzes the cause and effect determination of such economic indicators as employment, inflation, government policies in economics, and the role of monetary policy in affecting economic activity. Creator of the famous "Lucas-Islands" model of monetary influence among consumers, he has earned a place of international respect from economists all over the world. Lucas remains an active researcher and economic theorist today.

Robert Mundell

Robert Mundell is another leading contemporary macroeconomist. A Professor at Columbia University, Mundell is a leading figure in the development of supply-side economics. He was awarded the Nobel Prize in Economics in 1999 for his overall contributions to economic theory.

Mundell pioneered theory on optimal currency areas, which reflected his interest in the role of currencies in the economic fluctuations of countries. This work established him as a expert on money and currency, and Mundell was active in the development of the Euro-dollar for the European Union. His work in advocating supply-side economics is well known, and he is known as a leading expert on the gold standard and its historical implications.

Mundell was hailed as a prophet when he accurately predicted the rampant inflation of the 1970's. He has developed several important economic models, including the Mundell-Fleming model and the Mundell-Tobin effect.

Finn Erling Kydland

A Norwegian economist who won the Nobel Prize in Economics in 2004 for his research and models of macroeconomic systems, Kydland currently holds a teaching position at the University of California. Kydland has immersed himself in the study of the impact of government economic policy over a period of years. His work on the understanding of the fluctuations of business cycles is classic, and he is regarded as a pioneer in applying mathematical models to the analysis of economic activity.

A leading thinker in political economy and macroeconomics, Kydand has done primary and secondary research in the effects of fiscal and monetary policy on business cycles. Labor economics is another specialty of his, and he is regarded as one of the most important of the labor economists. The relationships between the availability, cost and demand for labor on economic cycles is a paramount interest of Kydland.

Edward Prescott

A major macroeconomist of the day is Edward Prescott. A close collaborator of Finn Kydland, with whom he shared the Nobel Prize in economics in 2004, Prescott currently serves as an economist for the Federal Reserve System.

Prescott has concentrated his economic interests in the areas of general equilibrium and fluctuations of economic activity. His particular field of interest is the role of central banks in applying monetary policy to affect business cycles. He addresses the question of whether central banks should be given wide ranging power to increase or decrease the money supply in an attempt to avoid economic extremes. Prescott developed the Hodrick-Prescott model of strategies to even the ups and downs of business cycles. This was widely hailed by economists as a major breakthrough in the management of economic fluctuations in an economy. Prescott currently engages in monetary and fiscal research as well as holding several teaching positions in economics.

Developmental economics

Developing countries have unique economic problems that more sophisticated economies do not. Particularly important is the area of long term economic growth in developing economies. This field is called developmental economics. It also includes the microeconomic analyses of individuals and firms in such fledgling economies.

A highly analytical field that uses econometrics (mathematical applications to economics) to predict economic patterns. Usually both mathematical and qualitative tools are used to measure and predict economic activity in developing countries. Included in the field is the problem of long term debt, and the action of international economic agencies such as the International Monetary Fund. The problem of encouraging and sustaining economic growth in such countries is a primary objective of economists. The field includes not only economic issues and tools, but also social and political methods to influence the whole society.

Political economy

Political economics is an umbrella term that includes a wide variety of economic approaches to study and predict behavior. It often uses techniques and tools from other social sciences in its applications. Political economy is a maverick in economic theory, as it often contravenes accepted economic doctrine. Interdisciplinary by definition, political economy studies the interactions of social and political factors on economic issues that affect markets.

- 47 -

The term originally was used in political science to compare and contrast relationships of geopolitics between countries. a number of political-social-economic schools have made political economy their main interest. The historical long term implications of political economy are of great interest to economic historians.

Scope of political economy

The economic activity and policy of the state is a major concern of political economy. Questions such as the level of unemployment, budget surpluses or deficits, and general economic well-being are all important concepts in political economy.

Political economy may be said to include all methods of production and distribution of excess funds or remedy of deficits in an economy. The importance of structural relationships in a society is the basis of political economy. The field of general economics places more importance on the allocation of scarce resources to satisfy unlimited demand. Political economy, because of its inclusion of social and political elements, is a broader field in a sense. The historical role of a country is very important in political economy. For example, the history of serfdom in Russia set the stage for Communism in the early part of the 20th century. American self-reliance and independence set a framework for capitalism to prosper. These historical precedents must be included in the study of political economy.

Capital

Capital is a comprehensive term for all or any methods by which products are made by labor. This includes a wide variety of tools or elements. Physical capital may include all categories of real objects such as equipment, plants, land, and machinery that contribute to the process of production. Intellectual capital is the necessary ingredient that transforms the production process by human interaction. Included in intellectual capital is the utilization of information, management skills, technological advances, and application of ideas and theories which are catalysts in the economic system.

Although capital is generally regarded as an essential ingredient of benign economic activity, it can also be used to foster the defense of a state or prepare a country for an aggressive war. The designation of large portions of Germany's capital was used to attempt to dominate Europe by the Nazis. Capital is commonly used to further a state's geopolitical aims through peaceful or belligerent goals. The utilization of capital is a prime indicator of any country's goals and ambitions.

Economy networks

Transportation is the network that allows the economy to function. Capital and labor must be moved to land in order to facilitate production. Finished goods must be moved through channels of distribution to be available to consumers. Transport is necessary for the movement of products, people, and capital.

Economic exchange is the basic activity of economics. The circular cycle of exchange from consumer to suppliers and back are the transactions that move an economy. The field of exchange is the marketplace, and money is the medium through which these transactions move. Building an infrastructure for market transactions is necessary to allow an orderly and dependable mechanism for economic exchange.

Consumption of goods, services, and ancillary products is the final activity for

- 48 -

satisfying the needs and wants of society. Consumption also may include the less tangible qualities of health, leisure activity, goodwill, and freedom of choice.

Disposal

All excess products of consumption or production must be eliminated as waste. The failure to dispose of these waste products will result in an impaired economy and a degrading of quality of life. Waste removal requires a large physical capacity and the employment of significant capital resources. The increasing urbanization of the world makes waste disposal an important priority.

Systems of waste removal include garbage and sewage operations as well as preventative measures of recycling and legislation to protect the environment. Governments must take responsibility for waste removal because of the scope of the problem. The ecological movement and "green" economics of the past 30 years have raised questions on the economics of waste and the quality of life. This has generated increased concern about such issues as destruction of natural habitats, global warming, air and water pollution, and the importance of sustaining our natural resources.

"The Market"

The central arena of political economy is the marketplace where economic activity occurs. It is also the intersecting point of the sometimes competing economic interests and forces at play. Common causes may be found by unlikely allies and groups may be pitted against each other for economic advantage. In a capitalistic economic system, the major task of the state is the creation and preservation of capital and the economic choices involved in its allocation.

Socialism maintains that decisions and implementation of production should be determined by the power of the state, ostensibly to create the greatest good for the most people. This philosophy brings socialism into conflict with capitalism that requires that fundamental economic power should be in private hands. Communism seeks control over all factors of production as well as political and social dominance over its society.

Adaptive expectations

When individuals base their expectations on past economic events and history, it is called "adaptive expectations". An example would be if the stock market has been strong for a period of time, the public will have positive expectations for future advances.

Individuals will base their future economic decisions on the cumulative past experience of recent economic activity. These decisions will become self fulfilling if consumers are pessimistic about the future of the economy. An example of adaptive expectations is the general attitude regarding inflation. In the United States, as well as most of the free world, inflation has become a fact of economic life. The expectation of rising prices, increasing wages, and general cost-of-living increases have bred a culture of inflationary expectation that rarely fails to materialize. Sometimes general pessimism about the economy serves as a deterrent to economic expansion. This is another example of adaptive expectations at work.

Balance of payments

The net sum of a country's exports and imports is known as the balance of payments for a country. These trade activities include finished products, raw materials, financial resources, and transfer payments. If the sum total of cash and liquid assets flowing into a country is greater than the outflow, the country has a positive balance of payments. If the opposite is the case, the country has a negative balance of payments.

International accounts include current accounts derived from the net flow of assets resulting from the trade of goods, services, and transfer payments. The accounting of funds received from sales and purchases of financial instruments is called a country's capital account. The foreign reserves account includes international funds, gold, and balances in exchange accounts. The sum of all these accounts determine the balance of payments for a country.

The Monetary System

As in other markets, the same elements of analysis may be used for the money market. The laws of demand and supply apply to the money market and result in market equilibrium for the price of money. The quantity of money in the system is also a product of these forces.

Money in circulation includes actual paper money and coins. Paper money may be banknotes or Federal Reserve notes that are physically produced by the United State's mint but represent money created by the Federal Reserve based on the credit of the federal government. This credit is electronically created by the government to influence the economy. In reality, since all paper money is based on the promise of the government to honor the currency, all notes are electronically produced. Coins may be produced outside of the Federal Reserve System by legislation. The total money supply is within the scope of the Federal Reserve System.

The money supply may be measured in a number of ways. Technically, money may be defined as anything that is used to pay a debt, but in practice money is defined as the currency and coins in circulation. Economic analysis of money uses symbols to designate different measurements of money.

The widest definition of money is as "a store of value." In the United States the Federal Reserve designates the definitions of money measured by various computations. The total of all coins and notes in circulation at any given time is designated by the notation MO. M1:MO represents all funds in circulation plus all checking and savings accounts (demand deposits). M2 adds to this money market funds and certificates of deposit held by all investors. M:3 includes all of the above forms of money measurement plus international funds and agreements to buy currencies. These definitions are helpful in monetary analysis by designating components of the money supply in various measurements.

Monetary exchange equation

One of the most widely used monetary analytical tools is the money exchange equation which provides a link between the money supply and inflation or deflation. Elements of the money exchange equation are the velocity of money - defined as the number of times money turns over; the Gross Domestic Product (value of all goods and services produced in a period); and the Gross Domestic Product Deflator, a measure of inflation in the economy.

Money Supply and Cash currently extant in the United States includes $1.4 trillion in coins and bank notes in circulation. Add to that certificates of deposits held by individuals and businesses and the M2 figure reaches $6.5 trillion. When you include all of the international balances and agreements to purchase currencies, the M3 number jumps to $9.7 trillion.

When this total is divided among all citizens of the United States the per capita figure is about $30,000 for each person.

Creation of money

The total money supply can only be increased (with the exception of coinage) by banks creating new funds through the Federal Reserve system through the electronic crediting process where notes are exchanged for electronic credits. The broader definitions of the money supply include demand deposits or checking and savings accounts, plus certificates of deposit.

Banks list demand deposits as their major assets. A fraction of these deposits may be loaned thus creating "new" money. That process may be repeated a number of times to expand the money supply. The Federal Reserve controls the amount of new money that can be created by setting a minimum reserve requirement for banks to hold against their total demand deposits. Raising the reserve requirement limits the amount of new money that can be created, while lowering the reserve requirement allows for an expansion of the money supply.

Function of bank reserves

To create additional funds in the money supply the central bank (The Federal Reserve in the United States) may buy a quantity of government securities on the open market thus increasing money available for banks to lend out under the fractional reserve system. This will increase the total money supply. To reduce the money supply the central bank sells government securities on the open market and depletes the funds in the private banks. In this manner the Federal Reserve maintains some control over the total money in circulation.

Summarizing the creation of money by central banks by buying Federal Reserve notes and silver certificates on the open market, placing more funds in the deposit accounts of private banks. Private banks, in turn, loan out a percentage of the funds which in effect creates new money. The funds may then be turned over or multiplied many times increasing the impact of the initial increase in money.

Money market instruments

There are a variety of money market securities or instruments available for trading.
- A common type is a draft or bill drawn on a bank which guarantees full payment of the amount. This is known as a "Banker's Acceptance".
- Promissory notes or drafts have a specific maturity date and are sold at a discount on the open market.
- Time deposits with specific maturity dates and a specified rate of interest are known as Certificates of Deposit.
- Short term government securities such as Treasury Bills are issued by various federal or quasi-federal agencies.
- Federal securities include deposits held by the Federal Reserve at any of their branches or agencies. These notes all carry an interest charge.
- Cities, towns, and counties often float short-term issues to finance specific projects or general operations..
- Treasury Bills are very short term securities issued by the Federal government and are traded on the open market.

Bank regulations

Since the failure of hundreds of banks during the great depression, the solvency of commercial banks has become a responsibility of government. Demand deposits are insured by agencies of the government so a depositor is protected from losing assets if a bank should fail. Of course, the major objective of banking regulation is to prevent failures.

To maintain the integrity of the banking system federal and state governments have required commercial banks to follow certain rules and regulations. The most important of these requirements is to insure banks reserve a certain percentage of their demand deposits as a reserve asset, insuring that banks do not overextend themselves with loans. Today only transaction deposits are subject to this rule. This regulation protects depositors against bank insolvency as does the federal governments insurance plans. The Federal Reserve imposes capital guidelines for commercial banks and savings banks which provide regulations on certain types of loans. These guidelines are risk-based and protect banks from making poor decisions on a borrower's ability to repay the loan.

Currency

Currency may be defined technically as any legal tender with which debts may be settled. Currency's major use is to facilitate the exchange of goods and services in the marketplace. The world is divided into "currency zones" which determine what currency may be used in trade. Rates of exchange are a market where different currencies may be bought and sold. Both bank notes and coins are considered currency. The country that issues the currency owns a monopoly in that market.

Central banks of countries are the institutions that control currency (and the money supply) through monetary and fiscal policy. These central banks or other monetary authorities (set up as an agency by the government) control and implement monetary policy and activity. Such authorities differ in their power from country to country. For example, in the United States

The Federal Reserve is a wholly independent agency free of political controls. Although Congress legislated the Federal Reserve into existence it remains completely independent in its activity.

Gold standard

A monetary system linked to the value of gold is said to be on the gold standard. Those who issue currency agree to exchange bank notes and coins for gold based on a fixed exchange rate. Thus gold becomes the basic unit of account to measure all wealth against. Gold standards were originally created to stabilize currencies by making it impossible for governments to create money at their pleasure. The gold standard also protects against hyper-inflation and the over-expansion of debt in an economy.

Originally, when the major form of money was coins (usually silver or gold) there was a logic to the gold standard. The gold standard was once a common phenomena among nations, but has now been replaced by systems giving the central banks of countries the power to create money and manipulate monetary policy for the good of the economy.
No modern country would return to the gold standard despite the protection it affords.

Gold was historically considered to be the ideal measure of wealth and a practical unit of account for market transactions. Gold was rare, easily measured and divided (originally by weight), extremely durable, and provided a uniform measure of value that transcended geographical boundaries making it ideal for settling debts between nations or individuals living in different areas. Gold may be easily transported and was used as a convenient base for the early banking systems in the world.

Bank notes and other forms of paper currencies have obvious practical advantages over gold. Besides providing central banks with the power to create money, paper currencies are portable, resistant to hoarding, and may now be transferred electronically for speed and simplicity. The complexity of the world economy made gold obsolete in the modern world except as an investment or reserve. International trade in the modern world could not be conducted with gold as the measure of value.

The central rationale for the gold standard is the theory that an increase in the money supply will cause inflation. If there is speculation over the value of money in the future, uncertainty will erode economic growth. Such uncertainty about the true value of money leads to a chaotic economy. The gold standard was implemented in most cases to stem this uncertainty. The gold standard would guarantee confidence in the economy, and benefit both domestic and international commerce.

A second reason for instituting the gold standard was to put stringent limits on the role of the central bank in controlling the economy. Governments were thought to be inept in economic affairs, and the gold standard insured a limit on their participation. The gold standard would also build confidence in money markets and inspire individuals and businesses to boost economic activity without fear of government intervention.

Today gold is held by nations to protect their currencies and provide a stable reserve of stored value in an economy. Gold tends to fluctuate with the rise and fall of the dollar on exchange markets. When the dollar depreciates in relation to other currencies, the value of gold rises. Thus gold serves as stable financial asset in the portfolios of almost all central banks in the world. It serves a type of internal reserve that may be called upon should adverse economic conditions arise. Banks may also use gold as a reserve against loans to their own governments as well as international trading partners.

Banks seek to hold in reserve assets with "real value" rather than electronically produced money. They may add real property, silver, and other stable assets to protect themselves. International banks also tend to hold significant amounts of United States dollars because of the stability inherent in the American economy. Central banks must feel they have stable assets to meet any economic crisis that might arise.

International Monetary Fund

The international financial network is a huge and complex array of associations and organizations representing governments, businesses, and individual. This includes a bewildering number of markets featuring ever changing exchange rates and fluctuating conditions in the world's economy. Overseeing and monitoring this system is the International Monetary Fund. The IMF stands by as a consultant and watchdog over exchange markets and the resulting balance of payments account of participating countries.

The IMF is made up of 184 countries, joining in a cooperative effort to control international markets and avoid financial instability. The institution has grown

- 53 -

dramatically since its inception when only 44 countries were included in the charter. Presently the IMF provides an important role in helping developing nations gain stable economies. Increased membership and the problems of new countries such as those created with the breakup of the Soviet Union have made the role of the IMF an increasingly important one in the world.

As may have been anticipated, the International Monetary Fund has become an object of criticism since its charter. One accusation is that the IMF has been partial toward countries who have friendly relations with the United States and other Western powers. Liberal and radical critics accuse the IMF of supporting countries with dictatorships and ignoring complaints regarding civil liberties and human rights in these nations.

Defenders of the IMF respond that the organization is an economic, not political group. They contend that before a democracy or republic can flourish, it must have a stable economy. The debate continues with liberal politicians supporting the pro-active policies of the IMF in stabilizing economies, while more conservative observers feel that supply side policy would allow the economies of developing nations to grow unimpeded by government intervention. The tendency of the IMF to promote currency devaluation is particularly aggravating to conservative economists and politicians alike.

The World Bank

The World Bank was chartered in 1944 when the post World War II devastation of economies was a major global concern. The organization addressed the problems of rebuilding the economies of Western Europe and provide stability for international investment in those

countries (as well as other developing nations). In recent decades, the World Bank has become an active participant in reducing poverty and promoting economic growth in third world countries. Included in the economic support is the improvement of education, farming, and manufacturing technology.

The major financial tool of the World Bank is to provide funds through loans to these countries. The loans usually carry a much lower interest rate than what normally would be charged. The World Bank is actually an association of five separate but related agencies working toward a common goal. It is highly regarded as an organization of integrity by economists and governments alike.

The work of the World Bank is to provide financial and consulting support for developing countries. The problems of dire poverty and famine are common in these countries, and the World Bank is active in attempting to solve these problems.

Tools of the World Bank are primarily financial, but the World Bank serves as an economic resource for financial planning for these countries. Funds are loaned at preferable interest rates to build or repair infrastructure of countries, as well as promote social and economic reforms. Environmental issues are important to the World Bank in making loans and supporting third world countries. A new emphasis on reducing poverty has influenced recent policy at the World Bank. This includes the advocacy for individual businesses to rebuild flagging economies. Broader goals have been related to the improvement of the standard of living through the promotion of reduced pollution, education, and the creation of entities capable of sustainable growth over time.

Although the World bank has a generally good reputation in global economics, it is not without its critics. The crux of these concerns is that many of their programs include provisions that alter the structure of the society and rob it of its autonomy. Almost always, the World Bank promotes economic liberation from archaic practices, which are sometimes deeply ingrained in the society of a country. These policies often reduce the power of a nation in managing its own economy, in the interest of promoting the general welfare.

Another related criticism of the World Bank is its liberal and progressive political stance. The Bank often requires countries to accept certain conditions as a requisite for financial aid. Sometimes, critics argue that these requirements include reforms not appropriate for unstable governments and countries in conflict. The influence of the United States is often thought to be excessive, and this causes policy that would favor American economic and political interests. Examples include the introduction of foreign businesses to compete with local industries.

Gresham's Law

When two or more types of money are commonly used in an economy, and each is assigned the same value by the country, problems may arise. Thomas Gresham, a 15th century English financial genius, stated that money that has a market value lower than its buying power will driveout a form of money that has stronger consumption value. People will tend to keep this "good money" as a store of value and spend the "bad money" to exchange for goods and services.

This situation can only happen if two different forms of money are in circulation and the state decrees them to have equal value, when in fact they do not. Given a choice of exchanging good or bad money for goods and services people will always spend the bad money and retain the good money. Thus as Gresham's law state, bad money will drive good money out of circulation. This becomes a serious economic problem if people are hoarding good money as a store of value and using bad money in the marketplace. Soon all the good money will disappear as people hoard it.

International Economics and Growth

Inflation

Inflation strikes when there is an general price increase of goods and services against one currency. Using a price index such as the Consumer Price Index as a measuring tool to compare prices at different times. A fictional "market basket" of commonly consumed staples is measured and charted over a period of time (usually one year). If the price of the representative market basket has gone up, inflation has occurred. For example if a typical basket costs $500 this year as compared to $400 last year for the same basket, inflation has risen over a year. Inflation reduces the buying power of money and if uncontrolled, can threaten the entire economy.

An example of runaway inflation occurred in Germany in the 1930's. Inflation was rampant and people literally had to take barrels of money to markets to exchange for goods and services. This rampant inflation helped bring the Nazis to power.

Deflation, the general lowering of prices and the subsequent increase in purchasing power of money is a much less frequent phenomenon.

Measuring inflation can be an inexact science because there are a number of price indexes that can be utilized. Most price indexes are based on information gleaned through government agencies and institutions. to accurately measure the rate of inflation, hypothetical market baskets of goods are compared from year to year. An adjustment termed a hedonic adjustment may be applied if there is a change in the makeup of the basket of goods. The weight given each product or service in the basket will affect the rate of inflation. The inflation rate is the percentage rate of price increase from one year to the next on identical bundles of goods.

The United States has suffered through some significant periods of inflation, particularly after World War II. Europe has been plagued with hyperinflation which is an extreme rise in prices due to the fall of the purchasing power of money. Such hyperinflation destabilizes economies and may result in a political and social crisis, as well as an economic one.

There are a number of indexes that may be used to chart the rise of inflation. Perhaps the most common one is the Cost-of-Living index which seeks to measure how much it actually costs an individual to live foe a specified period of time. This index is measured by the Consumer Price Index, which prices bundles of goods and services and compares them over time.

Another reliable measuring tool is the Producer Price Index which accounts for the actual amount of money the producer of goods and services receives. This is a net figure that considers other economic realities such as taxes in the computation. Commodity price indexes focus on changes in prices of essential commodities used in an economy. it is widely used in agricultural economics.

There are indexes that measure price changes in products sold by wholesalers, which are then passed on to retailers for sale to consumers. Some indexes attempt to pinpoint the personal consumption of individuals, but this is difficult to do with any degree of accuracy.

The "Misery Index" was developed to measure the economic hardships of combined unemployment and inflation. Although controversial, this index attempts to ascertain the level of economic impact on citizens in a society beset with the twin problems of inflation and unemployment. Economists have not been able to agree on the effect of such an index on individuals or businesses.

There is a school of thought that argues that previous histories of inflation linked to economic unhappiness has conditioned the public to regard any increase in inflation to be cause for concern. For example, a relatively low level of rising prices may have a psychological impact beyond the economic one. Some inflation is considered necessary to balance the business cycle during periods of recession. One could say that the public takes a much dimmer view of inflation than do economists. This difference becomes important if the public reacts negatively to minor inflation and it becomes an expectation of a weakened economy.

Pinpointing the causes of inflation is an area of controversy. Monetary theory holds that inflation is a direct result of an increase in the money supply without a corresponding growth of the entire economy. In the simplest terms, this means the amount of money available for consumption will be the prime determinant of spending in the economy.

Neo-Keynesian economists feel that the injection into the economy of large expenditures by government and its agencies as a goad to economic growth.

They posit the theory of demand-pull inflation where the demand by consumers for goods and services and the inability of the economy to respond to increased demand cause prices to rise. Cost-push inflation is the result of a sudden and unexpected increase in the cost of an essential product or service. Some believe that inflation is a permanent feature of a modern economy, where guaranteed wage increases and adaptive economic behavior based on past history insure some level of inflation will occur regularly in an economy.

Most modern countries are in a constant struggle with inflation. There are several strategies employed to keep price increases at an acceptable level. Monetary policy gives central banks the power to fight inflation by applying monetary policy and most importantly, by setting interest rates. When inflation threatens an economy, the raising of interest rates acts as a deterrent to price increases by making money more costly and slowing the economic activity of a country. Central banks have the autonomy to apply these measures when they feel they are appropriate.

An imposition of wage and price controls is a more drastic way to slow or halt inflation. These measures have many drawbacks, including the possibility of depressing the economy too far. Controls also promote hoarding, artificial shortages, and sometimes encourage the creation of alternative marketplaces that impair economic growth.

Hyperinflation

Runaway or hyperinflation is an economic crisis in which prices rise at an alarming rate while currency becomes devalued. There are no accurate measurements for hyperinflation, but economists agree a general and rapid raising of prices without a corresponding

movement toward equilibrium is a recipe for runaway inflation. True hyperinflation is recognized when governments are forced to dramatically increase the money supply as currency loses value.

Most hyperinflation is created by the printing of vast quantities of paper money to attempt to react to price increases. This usually initiates a spiral of increasing prices and decreasing value of the currency. This cycle is difficult to break because expectations of individuals and businesses are for yet more rising prices and devalued money. A common reaction to hyperinflation is the use of hard money as a store of value and medium of exchange.

Stagflation

When high inflation is joined by a depressed economy and high unemployment, the result has been called "stagflation."

Unexpected changes to an aggregate supply can create an economic trauma that has implications for the entire economy. Stagflation creates a dilemma for central banks. If the bank chooses to stimulate the economy by lowering the reserve requirements for commercial banks and reducing the interest rates it runs the risk of generating too much money which will increase inflation. Should the bank elect to combat inflation by raising the interest rates and the reserve requirement of banks, these actions could depress the economy further and result in more unemployment. Both choices have significant negative results for a struggling economy.

When the United States faced this dilemma in the 1970's, it was thought to have been caused by the failure of the government to gauge prices. The ultimate

- 57 -

response to this period of stagflation was the emergence of supply-side economics as a strategic tool. Economists disagree on the effectiveness of this strategy.

History of money

Money has been defined as any store of value which has intrinsic value or is a representation of a store of value (bank notes). Money is the lifeblood of market transactions, serving as a measure of value, a medium of exchange, and as an accounting convention.

As a means to exchange value for goods and services money has no peer. But for this to be the case, money must have a guaranteed and obvious value of its own. Historically, commodities including crops and livestock were the first forms of money. When money became accepted as a representation of commodities, the market system was revolutionized. It made simple trading and quickly became an accepted medium of exchange. In earlier times, money represented the commodities of precious metals, notably gold and silver. In modern economies, money depends on the guarantee of the government to honor its value. These guarantees permit international trade without risk about the value of the money involved.

The first "money" were commodities that were traded under a barter system. The next advance in the form of money was the minting of coins of precious metals, usually silver and gold. This form of money had intrinsic value but was a very limited resource. It could be transported fairly easily in moderate amounts, and was difficult to forge. The next leap in the form of money was the advent of paper notes, issued and guaranteed by governments. In modern economies money has taken on a variety of new forms, some a result of increasing technological advances.

Modern economies feature paper notes backed by the central bank and government who issues them. Coins with a small percentage of silver or gold are also assets honored by central banks. The intrinsic value of precious metals in most coins is negligible. By far the most revolutionary change in the form of money has occurred in the last 100 years. Demand deposits, credit cards, commercial paper, certificates of deposit, mortgages, and public and private promissory notes are all forms of money today.

Qualities of money

All money or forms of exchange share common characteristics which define the store of value of the currency used. Money must be a generally accepted medium for trading and settling debts. Acceptance of money depends trust in the issuing institution or nation.

To be useful as a deferred payment instrument, money must serve as a basic unit of account in an economic system. This requisite is fulfilled if money is seen to be a standard of value through which other goods may be given comparative value. The relative cost of any good or service must be measured against a standard which is the value of money. Perhaps most importantly, money must be accepted a store of value by everyone in an economy. In this manenr, money is a representation of the essential worth of any traded good or service. The system of deferred payment under which most markets operate make it imperative that money has its own essential store of value resting on the promise of a central bank or nation to honor the currency.

Effects of money

Money is an essential element in economics and forms the basis for individual, business, and government markets. Both the quality and the quantity of money affects the economy in fundamental ways. Central banks manipulate money quantities in order to influence the economy by expanding or contracting available funds. Monetary policies of nations have an important impact on the economies of those countries. It can be used to stimulate growth or to slow an overheated economy.

Monetary failure in a economy produces uncertainty and chaotic markets. When the USSR dissolved in the early 1990's a financial crisis occurred that still impacts nations. Defining money in the modern world can be difficult due to the myriad forms of credit available globally. The revolution started by credit cards in the last 50 years has completely changed the nature of exchange in most markets. Money has many substitutes, including demand deposits, savings accounts, credit and debit cards which serve as a store of value that is generally accepted.

Shrinking the money supply

Sometimes monetary policy demands reducing the quantity of money available in the economy. Central banks have the power to destroy or remove from circulation coins and paper currency at its discretion. Only a small fraction of the total money supply is represented by coins and notes.

Money is destroyed when government securities are purchased and when debt is paid off or canceled. Buying government bonds or other federal or state notes and paper takes that money out of the system. If a debt is paid to an institution such as a commercial bank, that money is lost from the total supply of funds. The Treasury of the United States is empowered to reduce the money supply through open market operations or retiring government debt.

When money is withdrawn from a bank, the money supply is reduced because the bank can no longer use the funds to loan and thereby create new money.

National income and output

National Income may be defined as the aggregate figure of all consumption, individual, business, and governmental, plus total investments and the balance of trade account for a country. This aggregate number, derived from adding these categories together, is called the expenditure method on national income determination.

Another calculation to determine the national income is to account for all the goods and services produced in a country during a fixed period. This is called the production accounting of national income. Yet another way of computing national income is to total all income received by individuals, businesses, and governments to arrive at total national income. This is the income approach to national income accounting.

To summarize, there are three ways of calculating national income: total expenditures, total value of production, and the aggregate consumption figures for a country.

GNP

The Gross National Product (GNP) is one of the prime indicators of the economic health of a country. Typically this aggregate figure of all goods and services produced in the economy for a specified period, usually one year. This computation uses "final" goods and services to reach the aggregate production. This means only final goods sold to consumers are included in this calculation. For example, raw materials produced and sold to manufacturers are not included if they are to be used to make final products that are then sold as final goods. GNP reflects only new final products for the measurement period are counted. Markets and transactions in used goods are omitted from GNP. Allocations of GNP are decided by the nation that owns the business unit, not where the goods are sold. For example, funds received from a Volvo manufactured and sold in the United States would be counted as part of Sweden's GNP as they are the owners of the corporation. This means that all proceeds of sales of final goods belong in the national account of the country that claims ownership of the firm that sold the goods.

A significant portion of Gross National Product is reserved and used for refurbishing and maintaining the productive capacity of a country. This includes monies used to repair and replace capital equipment that have become obsolete or less efficient. This total depreciation is the amount of GNP reserved for replacement and service of capital goods.

The national income approach is a calculation is the total income earned in a period, minus depreciation, indirect taxes, and direct taxes. Personal income, a major component of the income method, is the net national income less taxes, retained earnings, and transfer payments by governments. Personal disposable income, the amount of income available for consumption, is the total personal income minus personal taxes and plus transfer payments.

It is useful for economists to break down categories in order to analyze the interactions and relationships between elements of income earned in a country.

GDP

Another important measure of economic health is Gross Domestic Product (GDP). This calculation aggregates all goods and services sold in a specified period but allocates monies determined by where the sale actually takes place, rather than what country owns the business. A Volvo automobile manufactured and sold in the United States would be included in the GNP of America because it was earned in the United States, even though the business owners are Swedish. It follows that to compute GNP from GDP the aggregate total of income from goods sold by other countries must be subtracted from GDP.

Gross Domestic Product is a strong indicator of the short-term health of an economy as it measures current aggregate production. It is not as reliable a measure for accounting for the sources, and allocations of a country's income. GDP is a better measure of the state of production in the short term. GNP is better when analyzing sources and uses of income.

National income and welfare

There are many ways to measure the welfare on an individual in an economy. Although non-economic issues affect welfare to a large degree, economic welfare can be measured mathematically. Dividing the total net disposable income by the total population gives an economic value to welfare. Using economic value as an indicator, there is a correlation between this figure and various other measures of welfare.

Some problems exist in any attempt to measure actual disposable income. There is a significant amount of unpaid economic activity, including domestic functions such as the care of children. Mothers who are "employed" in childcare and running homes are not included in national income, which is an obvious flaw in the calculation.

Other factors important to welfare are the quality of life which includes social well being, freedom from ecological pollution, and political and religious choice. These factors are only indirectly measured in the welfare of individuals in a society.

National income and product accounts

The accounting for National Income uses traditional accounting procedures to report the state of the economy measured by aggregate income. Both businesses and government resources are used to prepare the reports. Typically, double entry bookkeeping practices are used in recording the economic information.

The left side of the report lists all earned income for the period, with salaries and wages the most dominant number in the account. The right side of the report summarizes production information, including consumption, investment, savings, transfer payments, and net exports (balance of trade). Totals for the two sides must be the same when all economic factors are considered. National income represents the total income of employees, government income, rental income, corporate income, and the net balance of transfer payments. Each of these categories are subject to specific defining qualities to insure the accounts are accurate.

Real and nominal values

In the analysis of Gross National Product there are inherent problems. Due to the presence of inflation, price levels rise virtually every year, leading to a rise in "nominal" increase in GNP even if there is no increase in production or income. This gives an unrealistic picture of GNP and paints an optimistic picture that is not entirely accurate. This figure is called "nominal" GNP. Real GNP is the nominal figure adjusted for inflation. If inflation is five percent, this figure must be applied to the total income or production figures to find real value.

An accurate computation of GNP must compare gross figures of income or production for two periods by designating values of goods and services after inflation. This real GNP is a much more accurate measurement of the growth and health of an economy. The higher the rate of inflation the larger the differential between nominal and real national income.

Wealth

The definition of wealth is both an objective and subjective one. In normal parlance, wealth is understood to consist primarily of money, land, and investments of an individual. However wealth includes many subjective factors that cannot be measured by strictly economic values. Additionally, concepts of wealth differ between cultures and societies.

Economic wealth must be measured in relation to all other individuals in the same economic systems. The income of an average middle-class American would make a third world citizen very wealthy. Within the United States, cost-of-living, income, and taxes vary widely. A wealthy person in Iowa may not be considered wealthy is Los Angeles because of differentials in the economic situations of the two places.

Additionally, intangibles such as environmental health, health of the individual, quality of life and dozens of other less objective factors all must be accounted for in considering real wealth.

Monetary policy

The managing of the economy by manipulating and adjusting the money supply is called monetary policy. Usually addressing specific goals, monetary policy includes adjusting prime interest rates, buying or selling government securities in open market operations, and setting reserve requirements for commercial banks. The higher the reserve requirement the less funds are available for expansion of the money supply.

Two major elements are in play in monetary policy - the amount of money in the economy, and the level of interest rates (the cost of using money). Monetary policy is geared to affect each of these variables in order to influence the economy. Monetary policy may be "easy." with lower interest rates and reserve requirements, or "tighter" with higher interest rates and higher reserve requirements. Monetary policy as a economic tool is favored by more conservative economists and politicians, while more liberal analysts prefer Keynesian methods stimulating aggregate demand.

The use of monetary policy as a major factor in influencing the economy is a fairly recent phenomena, beginning in the 18th century, and becoming a common strategy since the 1950's. Originally monetary policy concerned itself with increasing or decreasing the supply of money in the economy. Now much more sophisticated methods involving a bevy of financial tools and types of interventions.

Monetary policy, in its broadest sense, includes both long and short term interest rates, the quality and quantity of credit available, and the purchase and sale of government securities. It seeks to deter government action to influence aggregate demand through injections of money into the economy. Monetary policy also influences exchange rates, the velocity of money in the economy, as well as the ownership of securities in the economy.

The most extreme position on monetary policy is a return to the gold standard. This is a minority position held by only a few fringe economists. To adopt the gold standard would severely limit other tools of monetary policy.

Some schools of economics that favor markets free of government "interference," object to any monetary policy as a distortion of the marketplace. The so called Austrian school of economics vehemently opposes monetary policy in any form.

Advocates of market freedom argue that "the invisible hand" of self- interest should determine economic activity. In a situation of a free market, consumers will decide, based on their perceived self-interest, whether to consume goods now or at a later time. This is referred to as a saver's "time presence." Consumption now would deplete savings and cause a rise in interest rates due to the increased demand for money. Deferring consumption lowers the interest rate by reducing the demand for money. Critics of monetary policy say that such policies do not accurately reflect consumers' preferences, as they are artificially manipulated. When consumer preferences are ignored, businesses will often mistake lowered rates with consumer confidence and make poor investment choices.

Trends in central banking

As monetary policy has become more pro-active in modern economies, more sophisticated tools have been employed to influence the economy. The monetary level could be changed only by relatively crude methods, particularly when the gold standard was in place. Now central banks are active in the sale and purchase of government long and short term securities provides a tool for expansion or contraction of the money supply. Purchasing government securities takes money out of the supply, while buying these instruments injects new money into the system. The other method used effectively by monetary policy is changing the reserve requirements for commercial banks. An increase in the reserve requirement contracts the supply of money by compelling banks to keep a higher percentage of demand deposits. A reduction of the reserve requirement allows commercial banks to lend out more funds, increasing the money supply. Interest rates may also be lowered on secured loans to banks. If the rate is lowered enough, commercial banks will borrow from the central bank and loan out these fund in turn.

Inflation targeting

Monetary policy may be used as a tool to limit inflation. This goal is attained by raising the rate of interest which tends to restrain economic growth and tighten money. The Federal Reserve chairman announces periodic reviews and incremental adjustments to the interest rates as deemed necessary for the health of the economy. When the rate of interest is raised, it will cost commercial banks more to borrow from the central bank, thus cooling the economy. Although the interest rates are determined by an independent agency, they are subject to both social and political influence.

In the United States, a committee of the Federal Reserve Bank monitors and adjust interest rates. Close attention is given to the economic information that indicates inflation is rising, falling, or steady. A defined goal of the central bank is to control inflation, therefore monitoring indicators in the economy is an ongoing task. Alan Greenspan, chairman of the Federal Reserve, has become a familiar public figure in his periodic appearances before Congress where he reports on the state of the economy.

Federal Reserve

An example of how money is created may be understood by following the flow of funds. Suppose someone deposits $100 in his or her commercial bank. Assuming a reserve requirement of 10% the commercial bank creates more money by lending the $90 to a qualified borrower. This increases the money supply by $ 190. the additional money may be used for consumption, savings, or investment.

A second example would be the purchase of government securities. If commercial paper is purchased from an individual for $100, that individual has an extra $100 to consume, save, or invest. In any case the amount of money in circulation has increased by $100.

When the Federal Reserve lowers interest rates both businesses and individuals are encouraged to borrow and consume. This tool has far reaching effects in managing the economy.

Savings

Technically, in economic theory, disposable income is either consumed or saved. The amount left over when goods and services have been purchased by consumers is considered to be savings. Other categories of saving include corporations retained earnings and a government surplus.

The definition of the term savings is subject to some various interpretations. Individuals who repay loans of any kind rather than consuming the income are really saving. Interest paid on loans is not savings, but must be accounted for as income by those who receive the interest.

A differentiation must be made between saving, which is to increase assets, and savings, which is one element of a person's total net worth. To save is an activity that results in additional net worth as a separate category. Although this may seem to be a differentiation without a difference, the terms have separate meanings in economic analysis, and should be understood in economic terms.

Investments

Investment and savings are two sides of the same coin. If a decision is made to save, the opportunity cost of consumption is sacrificed. Savings can be utilized to reinvest in land, capital improvements, and equipment. This type of saving increases the total capita and promotes economic expansion.

Savings does not automatically equal investment, because both of these decisions are made by different entities in an economy, and often for different purposes. It is possible to save yet not increase investment, which can result in a decline in demand, which further leads to increased unemployment, reduction in production, and a business cycle that can lead to recession or depression. This has been named the paradox of thrift, because saving more would seem to be a positive spur to the economy, while in many cases it is not. However when investment increases over savings, aggregate demand is stimulated and the business cycle may turn toward expansion.

Although investment has a technical meaning in economic theory, it has several other definitions that apply to aspects of finance and economics. In everyday language, we speak of investment as a speculation for future gain. Common types of investments are stocks, bonds, government securities, mutual funds, insurance policies, commodities, and real estate.

Markets exist in many forms for various types of investments. Formal exchanges are the rule in security investing, examples including the New York Stock Exchange and the American Stock Exchange. Investments such as stocks and bonds may provide income in interest and dividends, and offer the promise of appreciation. Less tangible markets exist for countless items, such as coins, stamps, and markets for professional athletes.

Trading in securities has become much easier through internet buying and selling. Investment clubs are common in society, and colleges and universities allow students to manage funds as part of their training.

Interest rates

There are several ways to view interest rates in economics. Interest is the cost of using money in formal analysis. It is the cost of using capital. Keynes felt that interest rates did not affect saving or investment, as had been believed by classical economists. Classical economics taught interest rates would adjust toward equilibrium, and directly influence savings and investment decisions.

As in most areas of economics, the demand for and the supply of money determine interest rates. The rate of interest will fluctuate depending on many economic variables.

Finance employs the term interest rates to designate a charge for borrowing money. Interest may also be considered a return on an investment, the interest rate determining the return. It is actually a rate of return on a capital investment. An investor rents money and is charged a percentage of the value of the investment as the cost of borrowing.

Economic growth

Although there are many ways to measure economic growth, the increase of the store of value is the common rule used in macroeconomic analysis. It may be understood as the aggregate wealth of an economic entity. A common calculation to determine economic growth is to measure the aggregate value of all goods and services that an economy produces. A true measurement of economic growth must discount inflation to be an accurate valuation. This is called real time measurement.

In formal economic analysis, economic growth is determined by the total production of an economy adjusted for price rises. Economists often use the term "gross domestic product" to evaluate growth. Per capita GDP may indicate the level of the individual well being of an individual in an economy. As we will see, per capita GDP does not account for all the factors that determine the well being of people in an economy.

Often economists involved in analysis and policy decisions work on the assumption that all growth is good, without regard to the social costs. From a strict economic perspective, almost all economic growth may be rationalized as worthwhile. Using these precepts, plans and policies that are damaging to the general welfare may be defended effectively. For example, opening natural habitats for exploration of fossil fuels seems to make economic sense given the demand for oil. The costs of such decisions is not always readily apparent, but over time degrades the quality of life.

Positive economic growth involves the consideration of social and environmental factors in making economic policy. a successful economy does little good if the quality of life declines as a result of the growth. Economies exist for and because of the people and social systems they serve. If they fail to improve the general welfare they have failed regardless of economic growth.

Several economic factors may interfere with equating GDP per capita with individual well being. A significant allocation of assets is used to combat the negative effects of economic growth such as destruction of natural habitats and air and water pollution. Economic growth increases such intangibles as the increase in commuting which effects quality of life. Perhaps most importantly, GDP does not account for a significant amount of domestic production such as child raising and homemaking. The money equivalents for these tasks are omitted from the GDP calculation. There are numerous markets that are left out of GDP, including black markets, criminal activity, and alternative economies. There is also no provision in GDP for volunteer activity, and "do it yourself" tasks such as home improvements and landscape management. All of these economic activities are omitted from the formal measurement of per capita GDP, and fail to give an accurate picture of individual well-being.

The "Limits to Growth" debate

Economic growth carries with it substantial costs, both measurable and intangible. Given a world of limited resources, economic growth includes the more rapid depletion of such resources. the combined effects of economic growth on air and water pollution is too great to be measured. The destruction of rainforests and extinction of plant and animal species at an unprecedented rate are added and sometimes hidden costs of economic growth. The combination of rapid growth and resource depletion may eventually stop economic growth completely. The introduction of new

- 65 -

technology has fueled the rate of economic growth in the world. This technology may also be able to allow growth without many of the negative results.

There are many social scientists and economists who contend growth must slow or stop in order to maintain a level of well being that is acceptable. Other put faith in the ability of mankind to innovate and adjust to allow growth without devastating consequences.

Welfare economics

The analysis of income distribution and its consequences is called welfare economics. This field uses microeconomic theory to measure the effectiveness of the economic system in improving the general welfare. Welfare economics takes as its starting point the individual, the most basic component of an economy. Careful analysis of individual economic behavior yields much clearer understanding of the macroeconomic picture of an economy.

How well the wants and needs of a society are met may be termed social welfare. It may be viewed as the aggregate sum of the welfare of all individuals in a society. Welfare can be measured by dollars or income, or more generally in terms of individual economic satisfaction. Two major components of welfare economics are economic efficiency, which considers the total wealth of a society, and income distribution, which focuses on how the wealth is allocated throughout the economy. Both are key indicators of the general welfare.

Income distribution and social welfare

Income distribution in an economy measures the patterns of the allocation of income among individuals and groups. In a sense, the distribution of income not only shows the income levels of individuals, but also weights the relative importance of them in an economy. To calculate the aggregate satisfaction of the economy as a whole, the utility of each member must be measured. Any measure has subjective elements that cannot be mathematically represented in a welfare economics analysis. Such a utility based measure treats everyone the same, there is no relative difference between a wealthy individual and a poor one. Only the satisfaction of each is measured in absolute terms.

The Maximum-Minimum function argues that when the members of society who have the least have the most relative welfare satisfaction, only then is the welfare function maximized. Any welfare policy or intervention should address those in the most need. Both of the above examples are extreme positions on social welfare theory. In the real world, policy usually falls somewhere in between the two.

Transfer payments

A transfer payment in economic jargon is any transfer of money from one element of an economy to another in which there is no expected reciprocal return. Examples of transfer payments abound in an economy. Social security transfers, disability and unemployment benefits, and any payment from a government agency for which the recipient does nothing are all forms of transfer payments. Scholarships and interest free loans are also transfer payments.

Transfer payments can also flow between levels of government. Federal disaster relief, subsidies of all kinds, and direct transfers of monies for a multitude of purposes fall into the category of transfer payments. Even state and local taxes are transfer payments in the sense that they are paid by businesses and individuals

- 66 -

without getting anything in direct return. Of course many of the state and municipal functions are providing an indirect return to taxpayers in the form of essential services rendered.

Capital

Historically, capital was considered to be physical equipment, machinery, plants, and other major investments used in manufacturing. The more modern concept of capital broadens the definition to include a wide range of assets that are utilized in the production process.

Financial capital, which represents the operating funds and monetary investment in a business or plant. Financial capital is often obtained by corporations through the issue of stock in exchange for funds. Natural resources such as oceans, forests, mountains, and rivers provide natural capital which may or may not be publicly owned.

Capital that is used to provide support systems for fundamental production processes and operating ability is sometimes termed infrastructural capital. Much of this type of capital is represented in plants and equipment.

The abilities and acumen gained from education and experience is sometimes referred to as human capital. This incorporates the many types of growth and development from what we call human resources.

Purchasing power parity

In international trade, or speculation in currency markets, there must be a tool that uses a common measurement to compare value. This tool is called purchasing power parity, which provides an estimate of the amount of goods and services that can be purchased with different currencies. This tool is handy for understanding comparative value and measuring living standards in different countries. Differences in income levels in countries, and fluctuations in price levels make purchasing power parity an important analytical tool when comparing the value of currencies.

In international trade, it is imperative to know the equivalent value of the two countries trading, so that each buyer and seller understands the purchasing power of the monies involved. Differences in prices, standard of living, production and consumption variables are considered in the purchasing power parity calculation. This avoids complex analyses of independent variables in each country.

Rational expectations

In macroeconomics, the concept of rational expectations is used to provide a model of the results of economic decisions. The theory of rational expectations was first posited in the early 1960's as a refined tool for understanding the results of proposed economic actions. This theory has proved exceptionally useful in evaluating macroeconomic trends in Keynesian economic theory. For example, a business may wish to make a pricing change in a product and needs to know how this would affect sales and income. The rational expectations model would project the impact of the price change on the business.

In a sense, rational expectations are an informed guess after considering all available economic information. The theory cannot make predictions about human behavior in the marketplace without assumptions to provide a frame of reference. Outcomes that are forecast using this model do not differ significantly from the state of market equilibrium. Rational expectation models form the foundations of efficient markets theory.

Unemployment

In economics, an unemployed person is one who has the will and capacity to work, but cannot find meaningful employment. The total number of unemployed as a ratio to the entire labor pool is the rate of unemployment. The measurement of people without jobs who are actively seeking work is very difficult. A number of methods for measuring unemployment are used, each with its own flaws and advantages. The comparison of unemployment between different countries is very inaccurate due to different definitions of unemployment and social structures of countries.

Unemployment has both significant costs to an economy and society but also provides some economic benefits. Depending on the perspective taken, unemployment at various levels will affect an economy in different ways. More conservative economists argue the marketplace will determine unemployment, while welfare economists call for government action in the field.

Unemployment has both social and economic costs to individuals and society. The psychological impact of being unemployed degrades self-esteem, creates a sense of purposelessness, and increases mental strain. The financial implications can impair family life, reduce the standard of living, and make it difficult for some to receive benefits such as health insurance and disability payments which are often part of an employment package.

When workers are unable to find appropriate positions for their level of training and education, they are sometimes forced to take inferior jobs. These individuals are said to be underemployed and are generally dissatisfied members of the work force. High unemployment has profound economic costs in many situations. It typically reflects low Gross Domestic Product which implies both inefficient use of resources and the failure of production to provide products that improve the general welfare.

The major benefit of unemployment is that it has a "cooling" effect on the economy and tends to restrict general inflation. Many economists feel that given the scarcity of natural resources and the environmental pollution associated with rapid economic growth, it is not possible to continue increasing Gross Domestic Product year after year. Unemployment is a restraint to such growth.

Welfare economists argue the burdens of slowing the economy should not fall on the poorest and least able to cope members of society. They believe improved technology and planned economic growth that considers environmental factors will allow modest, healthy growth with low unemployment.

In any economy there is a certain number of the work force moving from job to job and seeking work they consider more appropriate to their skills. This common type of unemployment is termed frictional unemployment.

Unemployment in a free market situation occurs only in capitalistic economic systems. In Fascism, Socialism, and Communism the factors of production, including labor, are under the direct control of the state. Historically, precapitalist societies such as feudalism formed the basis for the economy. In this case the serfs were all employed (if able) by dictate of the Lords. More primitive societies such as tribes view the entire group as part of one family, and take responsibility for insuring all are cared for adequately.

Debate continues on the necessary and appropriate action of governments in curbing unemployment. Liberal and welfare economists often call for a more active role for government in increasing employment, while more conservative analysts feel government intervention exacerbates the problem by its interference. Laws forbidding strikes and layoffs are cited as inappropriate government action to solve unemployment.

There are several types of unemployment recognized by economists. Cyclical unemployment results in recessionary periods of the business cycle when aggregate demand falls. When there is a major change in structure or skill level of an industry unemployment may result. The advent of computers for word processing made typewriters virtually obsolete, causing those who make, sell, and repair typewriters to be unemployed.

Changes in the market due to shifting demand for certain products affect the employees who produce those goods. If demand for typewriters falls, demand for labor involved with typewriter production and sale also drops. This is also an example of unemployment caused by technological advances. Another type of unemployment is seasonal unemployment where productive activity in an industry is limited to certain times of the year. Commercial harvesting of oysters is a seasonal position.

Measuring unemployment in the United States is done with statistics and data obtained by the U.S. Bureau of Labor Statistics. Most countries have a similar agency providing this service. The major criterion for determining if an individual was gainfully employed during the weekly measuring period is straightforward. People are deemed to have been employed if they did any activity for pay or profit during the

period. Included in this group are temporary workers and seasonal employees.

Included in this calculation of employment are those who do hold jobs but were unable to work because of personal obligations, holidays, sickness, labor strikes or lock-outs, inclement weather or temporary maternity or paternity reasons.

Homemakers, students, and those imprisoned are excluded from the calculation of the employed. Individuals are classified as unemployed if they have actively sought work in the previous month and are ready and able to be employed.

Recessions

The technical definition of a recession is when a nation's real Gross Domestic Product decreases in two or more consecutive quarters of the fiscal year. Typically, recessions involve falling aggregate demand which causes prices to fall and economic activity to slow. It sometimes occurs when inflation rises quickly, and is combined with a slowing economy. This condition is called "stagflation." In general, recessions are characterized by falling prices.

Recessions appear in a more or less regular pattern in capitalistic economies. Recent patterns have indicated a recession may be expected every five to ten years. Most recessions are caused by lack of consumer and business confidence in the future.

Some economists encourage government intervention in a recession, while others feel such interference only adds to the problem. The latter group are more conservative economists who prefer to let the market determine the level of economic activity.

The Depression in the United States

Only once has the United States gone through a massive depression. In the 1920's, massive speculation and investment in stocks caused their prices to rise far above their true value. Adding to the problem was the fact that many of the stocks were purchased on credit, using securities as collateral. When the economy began to contract, share prices fell dramatically and the collateral supporting other stock purchases became worthless. The loans were called, became uncollectible, and triggered a financial panic that led to multiple failures in the banking system. Savings were lost, unemployment soared, and the economy spiraled into a depression.

After the election of Franklin Roosevelt in 1932, massiveinjections of funds were fueled into the economy. Precautions against future bank failures were addressed by federal insurance programs, and speculation in the stock market was regulated as well. Although these measures helped the economy, it was not until the United States entered World War II that it emerged from the effects of the depression.

The multiplier effect

The multiplier effect is a phenomenon that explains how a single injection of funds into an economy may cause an effect far beyond what might be anticipated. The multiplier effect is a analytical tool favored by Keynesian economists to advance their theories of increasing aggregate demand. For example, a decision to build a new shopping center has a much bigger impact on the economy than indicated in the single transaction. Builders will be hired, retail stores will open, restaurants and

theatres may flourish, all creating jobs and income that far outweigh the initial investment in the shopping center. The multiplier effect is seen most clearly in economic situations where there are significant unused resources in the economy that may be engaged by an investment of capital. This investment is said to increase incomes. demand, and employment, and give a general boost to the economy. Not all schools of economics recognize the multiplier effect equally, but it has become a standard tool in modern economics.

The accelerator effect

The accelerator effect is a hypothetical theory that posits that the general economic condition will have a major impact on private investment in the economy. The sequence of events may occur as follows; As Gross Domestic Product rises business confidence increases with the expectation of increasing sales, income, profit, and more efficient use of existing resources. The expansion spiral may continue as businesses increase investment and employment, and workers incomes and consumption also rise. The multiplier effect can accelerate all of these economic indicators, causing yet more expansion.

The accelerator effect may also be seen in a contracting economy. As economic activity slows, businesses cut employment and investment in anticipation of reduced profits. These effects are all accelerated and the downward spiral of the economy is exacerbated. If unchecked, this deflationary spiral may lead to a recession, or in the worst case, a depression.

Economic cycles

Cycles of expansion and contraction of economic activity seen regularly in economies are called business (or economic) cycles. The expansion or contraction tends to occur across the board in almost all areas of economic activity, contributing to the impact and intensified by the accelerator concept. Standard measurements of economic activity are increases or decreases in the real Gross Domestic Product.

Although there are definite patterns of economic cycles, they cannot be predicted accurately because of multiple factors affecting the economy. Cycles tend to have their own lifespan, and there is a debate as to whether government interventions are useful in smoothing out the fluctuations. An area of current research in economics is an investigation of the mechanisms that apparently trigger such fluctuations and can be identified and manipulated. The prediction of economic cycles has become a major factor in business, social, and political arenas.

Consumption

When a resource is used and eliminated, it has been consumed. Consumption is an important feature of economics, usually meaning personal consumption of goods and services. Consumption has its own determinants, including economic expectations, level of disposable income, and the propensity to consume. Ultimately consumption is a component of aggregate demand in economic theory.

Economics makes a clear distinction between production, the supplying of goods and services, and the consumption, or use of these goods and services. economic research into consumption raises the questions regarding the motivation and reasons for various levels of consumption. The relatively recent importance of our consumer society has placed this element of economic theory under the microscope of analysis.

Consumption in all its forms has developed a significant impact on the lives of everyone in a modern economy.

Green economics

Green economics is a general term that includes economics as one part of the total ecological system. It is an interdisciplinary branch of economics, including contributions from the social sciences, biology, and economics. There cannot be said to be a single school of green economics, but rather a loose confederation of movements, ideas, schools, and theorists. Green economics has elements of many social activists of today in its ranks.

A general mission statement for green economics is that the economy is one element in the ecosystem, and the ecosystem plays an important role in economic decisions. The concept of scarce resources is central to green economics, as is the idea of sustainable resources. Given the agreement that all resources are limited in a sense, green economics advocates moderate economic growth, with ecologically sound principles, that maintain rather than consume our limited resources.

Government

Any obligation owed by local, state, or federal governments is considered government debt. Such a debt is actually an indirect debt of the taxpayers as a whole, though it is seldom understood this way. Debt is most often incurred by issuing securities, primarily bonds, with varying lengths of maturity. Debt that is owed to citizens of the country incurring the obligation, is known as internal debt. However debt held by individuals, institutions, and governments from another country is called external debt. Although the great majority of government debt in incurred by notes and

- 71 -

bonds, some governments may borrow from central or commercial banks,

Fiscal conservatives rail against public debt while more liberal economists and politicians support raising funds for social welfare and defense. The issue of United States public debt, also called the deficit, has become an issue in politics and welfare economics.

Economic models

In economics, as in other disciplines, models are constructed simulations of actual problems in order to test a set of variables. Models provide a framework that clearly illustrates the change in economic elements when different variables are applied.

In economics, a model is a theoretical construct that represents economic processes by a set of variables and a set of logical and quantitative relationships between them. As in other fields, models are simplified frameworks designed to illuminate complex processes. Economic models are widely used in academic settings and in economic research.

Business uses economic models to plan and allocate resources as well as predict the impact of economic actions. Governments use models of the economy to plan policies and to justify implementation of economic decisions. Models are also useful in predicting future economic activity.

Econometrics

A collection of mathematical and statistical tools used in advanced economic theory are given the general name of econometrics. Econometrics is used extensively in economic research and in the creation of economic models. Econometrics allows researchers to place numerical values on economic concepts, and verify posited hypotheses.

An example of a widely used econometric formula is regression analysis.

When econometrics is used to study a variable over a specified span of time it is referred to as a time-series analysis. An example would be the impact of savings in the business cycle for the past 30 years. When econometrics is employed to measure different variables at one point in time it is termed cross-sectional analysis. Both time-series and cross-sectional analysis are used extensively in economic modeling.

Labor economics

As in all the factors of production, labor has a separate market based on supply and demand. The interaction between employers and workers is the frame of reference of labor economics. These interactions affect labor economics and determine income, employment, and wage levels. Labor economics is a vital field since most countries include maximized employment as an economic priority.

When labor economics is studied through the individuals and their role in labor markets, microeconomic methods are used.

The larger interactions between labor markets and the demand for goods and services, production, consumption, and investment fall under macroeconomic analysis. Both are necessary and useful methods for evaluating the role that labor plays in economic activity. Most of us are more aware of the macroeconomics of labor which tends to be in the news more often as trends of unemployment and productivity.

Labor market terms

Macroeconomics of the labor market starts with a series of definitions calculated from labor statistics.
- The labor force includes all people in an economy who have jobs or are actively seeking employment.
- To find the participation rate on individuals in the work force, the aggregate number of the labor pool is divided by the size of the total population.
- The unemployment rate is calculated as a percentage of those unemployed, but seeking jobs relative to the total population.

From these basic definitions, we can obtain stock variables, which measure a level at a particular point in time. Flow variables, on the other hand, are used to measure a variable over a specified period of time. Examples of flow variables include modifications of the labor market due to net entries and exits from the labor pool. This would include retirees, net immigration of eligible laborers, forced unemployment and frictional unemployment. these are flow variables that may be studied over any length of time.

Factors of production

Resources that are used in the production and manufacture of goods and services are called factors of production. They include land and natural products derived from land including dirt, gems, minerals, and fodder. The cost of using land is usually rent in one form or another.

Labor is another factor of production and this is a blanket term for all individuals involved in the manufacturing, marketing, and transfer of goods and services. The payment for labor is designated as wages.

Capital is the third essential factor of production and includes all products that are utilized in the making of final products, including physical plants, equipment, machinery and human expertise.

These definitions of the factors of production are from classical economics and political economy, and they remain accurate today although the idea of capital has been expanded to include human expertise and technology.

Balance of payments

The measurement of a nation's trade productivity is the net of the imports and exports of finances, services, and finished goods in international trade with other countries. Financial capital and transfer payments also enter into the calculation. Each country has three accounts to measure international trade activity.

The current account of a country has three components- the transfer account (for unilateral tranfers), the income account (measuring net income received from international transactions), and the trade account (a record of goods and services traded abroad).

The capital account indicates the net gain or loss in capital obtained from international trade. This is primarily used for cash and financial paper, including loans, investments, and savings. Finally the unilateral transfer account note all transfers of asset for which there is no compensation.

Each account may either have a surplus indicating the country gained more than they lost in that account, or a deficit noting the net loss for the country. The net total of all accounts gives a balance of payments figure for that period.

Commodity markets

Commodities are raw or unfinished components of finished goods yet to be produced. Agricultural products such as soy beans, cotton, and wheat are commodities. Separate markets exist for almost all commodities. Currencies of various countries are also traded as commodities in their own markets. Futures markets exist on many heavily traded commodities, where speculation fuels trading for future delivery of products paid for now.

Commodities were one of the first class of goods traded between countries. Modern commodity markets have been safeguarded by a bevy of rules and regulations insuring prompt and accurate payment between countries. International agencies, such as the Bank for International Settlements regulate transaction settlements, insure currencies, set reserve requirements, and generally reduce risks in trade inherent between countries.

Subsidies

In economics, a subsidy is a unilateral transfer of money, usually by a government institution, artificially supporting the price of a commodity based on the importance of that good to the general welfare. Subsidies take various forms, including direct cash payments, letters of credit, or tax incentives.

Subsidies guarantee the producer a better price than may be obtained on the open market. They correspondingly reduce the consumer price, but at a cost to the free operation of the market. Subsidies skew demand and supply curves, and encourage consumers to spend rather than save. This hurts the economy, and the consumers by causing overconsumption because of an artificially lower price. Subsidies have historically been used for agricultural products, particularly under governments attempting to increase income to producers. Subsidies were used heavily during the "New Deal" and "Fair Deal" to help selected groups in the economy.

Standard of deferred payments

In any transaction, there must be a currency or commodity that is generally accepted as a means of settling debt. Deferred payment for current transaction to be settled later are guided by the standard used at the time. Historically, gold and silver were used as the standard of deferred payments, because they had intrinsic value and everyone could agree on their worth. When the gold standard was in effect, all currencies were guaranteed to be exchanged at a fixed rate.

In modern economics, the strongest currencies usually serve as the standard of deferred payment. Today, the United States dollar and the European Union's Euro are considered the most reliable standard of deferred payment. Illegal transactions rarely allow deferred payments, but if they do compensation may be made in gold or diamonds, whose store of value is unquestioned.

The instability of money at a given time makes the deferred standard of payment more important.

Store of value

Any form of money or capital including commodities may be seen as a store of value if it meets certain standards. Any store of value must be readily stored, retrieved, and saved. The store of value must retain its value over time, both as intrinsic wealth and the ability to use it to settle debts.

Many assets have been used as a store of value over the centuries. Precious metals, primarily gold and silver have been historical favorites. The most stable currencies extant at a historical point also may serve as a store of value. When the British Empire was powerful, the pound sterling was often used as the store of value. real estate has always been known as a reliable store of value, and art, antiques, and rare collections have served this purpose.

Many of these are not practical for daily trading which includes immediate settling of accounts. The common feature is that they all have intrinsic value and rarely lose it. There is always a more or less stable demand for these items.

Okun's Law

Arthur Okun, an American economist, noted that changing unemployment rates had a significant impact on real Gross Domestic Product. Okun's Law seeks to describe this relationship. It may be summarized by stating each percentage drop in the unemployment rate results in a disproportionate rise in real Gross Domestic Product for the period measured. This observation made by Okun, is based on observable empirical evidence rather than on extensive economic research and econometrics.

The generally accepted ratio of Okun's Law is that for every one percent of increased employment there is a corresponding increase in real Gross Domestic Product of two to four percent. The significance of Okem's Law is the importance of increased employment in generating national wealth. It is often used to support economic policy which seeks to reduce unemployment and thus boost real GDP.

Macroeconomic models

A macroeconomic model is a simulation of the forces in a macro-economy. such models serve primarily to better understand the relationships under different variable of such macroeconomic measurements as total production, price behavior, level of employment of available resources, and total earned income.

These models are used to set up hypothetical economic situations that test the effect of economic action on other variables in the model. Primarily used for forecasting future economic conditions, they are used in economic research at academic institutions, government agencies and institutions, and independent economic consulting groups.

The first macroeconomic models were developed after World War II in Holland and the United States. A global macroeconomic model was conceived by economist Lawrence Klein who was awarded the Nobel Prize in Economics for his work.

The Laffer Curve

An important economic tool is called the Laffer Curve, which posits that government may maximize tax revenue by setting tax rates at the apex of this curve, and that any additional tax increases actually reduce tax revenues. developed by the economist Arthur Laffer, it is often used to justify tax cutting policy popular with conservative and supply-side economists.

The concept may be clarified by examining the extremes of zero taxation and a 100% tax rate. At zero taxation of course the government receives no tax revenue at all. At 100% tax rates the government also receives no tax revenue because there is no economic incentive to work, if all earned monies are collected as taxes. At some point between the two extremes is the tax rate which will secure the maximum revenue through tax receipts. Much of this is economic theory is not proved in the real economic world. The curve will also vary from country to country due to different economic environments., which may skew the Laffer curve in unpredictable ways.

High technology economics

Many economists and investors feel the sector of the economy using cutting edge high technological methods is the most promising for economic growth. This conclusion has promoted increased and sometimes speculative investment in high tech fields. But as we learned from the anticipated boom in information technology, reality does not always meet expectations. The so called "dot-com" boom in the last 20 years saw the making of great fortunes but also the loss of investments when companies failed to meet their expected growth. High technology economics still offers uncommon rewards for the astute investor, but must also be regarded as very high risk for investors.

Areas usually associated with high technology advances include nanotechnology, information technology, and biotechnology, among many others. High technology industries flourish across the world, making constant progress in developing new techniques and applications for multiple growth industries.

"The Invisible Hand"

One of the fundamental concepts of classical economics is the "invisible guiding hand of self-interest" that posits each individual will make economic decisions based on his or her best interests. Developed by Adam Smith, the father of capitalism and leading classical economist, the theory states that individuals acting in their own self interest will also promote the general welfare of all members of the society. Smith felt this was a social mechanism that tended to benefit all.

Smith's argument was based on his belief that in a free market economy, people tend to produce goods in demand by consumers. He did no necessarily feel all self-interested action by itself benefited all of society. Smith's original observations and conclusions are a foundation of classical economics, and has been incorporated in one form or another in many schools of economics. Much of macroeconomic theory uses the invisible hand concept in postulating economic behavior.

"Cost-Of-Production Theory of Value"

The concept that the value of an object represents the sum total of all the resources that were involved in producing it is called the cost-of-production theory of value. This cost would include any and all of the factors of production utilized in producing the good, Classical economists support the labor theory-of-value ideas of Adam Smith, David Ricardo, and Karl Marx. Marxs's theory is flawed by his inclusion of the surplus component of value unrelated to the production process.

Most contemporary economists reject the cost-of-production theory of value in favor of the marginal theory of value which contends that an economic value is determined by the marginal utility derived by the consumer of using the product. Some economists distinguish between sectors with cost-determined prices and values, and demand-determined value which is set by the level of aggregate demand.

Economic indicators

Business or economic indicators are specific measurements that are used to predict the future course of the economy. They are used as analytical tools to measure and forecast economic activity and future behavior of the economy. Among common economic indicators used are various indexes, compilations of data, summaries of economic activity in a period of time, and statistics measuring the level of consumption, investment, savings, and unemployment in the economy. Fluctuations in the money supply and industrial output are important indicators. Measurements for inflation, retail sales and stock market prices provide supporting data.

The National Bureau of Economic Research, whose prime interest is in predicting business cycle, provides many of the important economic indicators used for forecasting. When an indicator occurs behind economic activity, it is called a lagging indicator. Indicators current with economic activity are known as coincident indicators.

"Laissez-Faire"

Laissez-Faire is derived from the French, meaning to "let do" indicating a hands off approach. Historically, the term was used by the physiocrats who demanded less governmental influence on international trade. It has become a catch-all phrase for allowing the market the freedom inherent in transactions, without outside influences. Classical economics found a supporter for laissez-faire in Adam Smith, although he had reservations about some aspects of the policy.

A broader definition of laissez-faire reflects a style of leadership which allows maximum freedom of individuals to act on their own initiative rather than following orders routinely. It empowers subordinates to make independent decisions and take action on their own.

Critics of laissez-faire economics point out the failures of lack of any control on economic affairs. The 1920's are sometimes cited as a period of lack of government safeguards that plunged the country into the Great Depression.

Information economics

The sub-branch of economics which deals with the use of information in making economic policy and decisions is called information economics. Information has unique qualities, being wildly inaccurate at times, easily accessible, and difficult to fully believe. A prime element in economic decisions, a lack of reliable information makes accurate and valid choices difficult at times. The branch of information economics studies the mechanisms of economic technology, the value of economic information and its applications, and the asymmetries of information in economics.

The market for information is unique. Information is presumably for sale to anyone who will buy it; it can be sold multiple times. Information has virtually no marginal cost to the buyer. It is easy to duplicate and may be resold many times over. Sometimes information is sold as a bundle. Various sources and pieces of information are combined and sold with or without commentary or suggestions.

Economic language and reasoning

The methodology of economics is not unlike other sciences. The first step is the collection of observed economic information collected without bias. These observations ideally have measurable values that give a measure of worth.

This information is collected and used in the creation of economic models illustrating relationships between economic variables. Examples of such relationships include price levels to consumption, and unemployment and national income.

These models may be simple organizational tools for data, or complex calculations of relationships between dynamic economic factors. Finally, taking the organized observed data and constructing a model, a generation of economic statistics should follow. These statistics will be drawn from a simulated economy or economic situation and may measure the impact of an economic action on all other variables in the model. This will provide the basis for making informed economic decisions from information gained in the simulation.

Economic policy

Economic policy refers to the broad planning and implementation of economic measures of the government in regulating and effecting economic activity. It includes wide areas of monetary and fiscal policy, and effects virtually every aspect of an economic system. Politics and social pressures play a major role in influencing economic policy. International agencies and institutions such as the World Bank may also play a part in determining economic policy.

Several general areas of economic policy may be identified:
- Fiscal policy and stance refers to the government deficit or surplus and the methods of financing government operations.
- Policies on taxation include changing tax regulations, enforcing tax codes, and the methodology of tax collection.
- Government spending for usual operations of the government and special allocations for natural disasters and war.
- Determining the amount of money in circulation.
- The determination of interest rates that fall under government control.
- International trade policy including tariffs, reciprocal trade arrangements, and trade treaties.
- The rules and regulations that apply to the banking system.

Goals and tools:
Governments and economies usually set goals for their economic plans and policy decisions. Goals are short-tern and long-term ones, and focus on big picture elements such as inflation control, employment levels, and economic growth rates. These policy goals are implemented with economic tools that include monetary and fiscal policy, increases or decreases in government spending, international trade practices, regulation of labor markets, and many additional methods. Often goals are not exclusively economic, as with defense and other areas of the general welfare.

A government must determine which short term goals are most important to its policy. It may be impossible to reduce inflation while promoting more employment at the same time. Governments are usually more successful with a few short term goals that work with each other to affect long term goals. A consistent policy approach to economic problems is essential to achieve economic goals.

Stabilization policy

When a major goal is the stabilization of the economy it may refer to two different things which require different policy and economic action. One area of stabilization that is common is the smoothing out of the business cycles to avoid extremes. This type of policy goal may be attained by a combination of monetary and fiscal policy in order to minimize economic fluctuations and avoid inflation or recession. Usually the actions implemented are counter-cyclical, balancing economic trends with a goal of a stable economy.

Occasionally, an unexpected economic crisis arises which demands immediate government action. Perhaps a trauma to the banking or securities markets have caused a short-term situation that requires government intervention to ease the situation.

In these cases both the government and central bank work in accord to remedy the situation, sometimes with the help of international economic agencies.

Fiscal policy

Fiscal policy is all economic activity by the government in collecting money to finance current operating expenses and unilateral transfer payments to its citizens. The money is also used for social services and programs to maintain and improve the infrastructure of the country. Primary means of raising funds is the collection of taxes from individuals and businesses, borrowing by issuing notes and bonds, and taxes on services. Fiscal policy can be used to prime the economy by injecting funds into the system in order to increase aggregator demand. Governments must pay interest on the bonds and bills they issue to raise funds. the maturity dates vary widely between short term treasury bills and longer terms U.S. bonds. Monies paid as interest is raised primarily by taxation.

Total net government debt is called the deficit and remains an issue of controversy for economists and politicians alike. This debt should be

devalued by the country's inflation rate to reflect an accurate figure.

Reaganomics

The term Reaganomics is an umbrella description of the economic policy of the Regan administration from 1980 -1988. These policies faced very high inflation rates and increasing unemployment together called stagflation. These dual problems were addressed by applying the principles of supply-side economics, combining tax reductions with decreased government spending. Liberal economists and politicians bemoaned the approach as helping the wealthy at the expense of middle and lower income individuals.

Supply-side economics attempts to encourage investment and expansion through tax cuts and austerity programs rather than stimulating demand. This is the idea of the "trickle down" approach of economic well being beginning at the top. The twin problems of inflation and unemployment were largely solved during the Reagan years. There is hot debate whether this was caused by economic policy or simply a turn in the business cycle.

Internal economic stabilizers

The economy has some built-in stabilizers to help smooth out the business cycles. Both tax revenue and transfer payments adjust automatically when the economy begins to contract. Income tax revenues fall because of a decrease in employment. Transfer payments increase as individuals use food stamps and other government aid programs to bolster their income.

This means that net disposable income is not totally dependent on the economy's level of production, and the transfer payments allow more consumption to

- 79 -

occur that might be anticipated. Safeguards are also built in the banking system by federal insurance programs, and the stock market operates with rules and regulations imposed to prevent another panic similar to the 1929 crash. The entire economy has become more stable as a result of government policy intended to avoid the extremes in the economic cycle.

Thomas Malthus

Thomas Malthus, the 18th century economist who named economics the "dismal science," felt that population would grow at a rate that people would starve, and the level of population would reach a subsistence level. Malthus's theories have been proved wrong in a large part of the developed world. but his predictions are accurate for many poor third world countries who suffer periodic famines. Industrialized countries have developed technologies to produce food to keep abreast of population growth, which has been slower by birth control methods. Developing countries with unchecked population explosions and inferior technology often cannot produce enough food to feed themselves. These countries must rely on international aid and relief agencies to provide the essentials of life. Much of the development of third world nations is geared to increasing food production and introducing methods to slow the population growth. These actions have had mixed success to date.

Equilibrium output

The equilibrium level of aggregate supply and aggregate demand in macroeconomics: The level of prices is an important determinant of equilibrium points. Aggregate demand reflects the total spending of individuals businesses, and governments as well as net balance of payment accounts. The price level in macroeconomics determines total spending because of its impact on interest rates, the amount of wealth in the economy, and the international trade implications in price changes. Increases in prices will push up interest rates which usually has a dampening effect on spending. The wealth of an economy decreases as prices fall, devaluing the assets in that society. Price changes can benefit a country whose prices remain stable, while their trading partners have a general increase in prices. Goods and services become cheaper to buy in the country with falling prices than in those with a stable price level. All of these factors work in concert to move an economy toward equilibrium.

Government intervention

Governments may manipulate price levels in a number of direct and indirect ways. They can directly affect level by imposing price ceilings or price floors, limiting the range of price fluctuations of a good or service. An example of price ceilings are rent controls that city governments impose on landlords in some metropolitan areas. The classic example of a price floor is the minimum wage requirements for labor in some economies. Governments may also affect aggregate demand and supply by different policies and intervention. Keynesian economists believe the responsibility for increasing aggregate demand in a contracting economy belongs to the government. Monetary theorists believe the level of economic activity is directly linked to the total supply of money in the economy and use monetary and fiscal policy to determine the increase or decrease in the money supply, and thus the level of prices. Subsidies are another means the government may use to artificially manipulate prices in an economy.

References

1. *The Wealth of Nations* - Adam Smith
    Description: The book is usually considered to be the beginning of modern economics. It begins with a discussion of the Industrial Revolution. Later it critiques the mercantilism and includes a synthesis of the emerging economic thinking of his time. It is mostly known due to the idea of The Invisible Hand which means that people will unintentionally improve their community through pursuit of their own wants and needs.
2. *Das Kapital* -Karl Marx
    Description: Das Kapital is a political-economic treatise by Karl Marx. The book is a critical analysis of capitalism and of the political economy practices during his time. Marx bases his work on that of the classical economists like Adam Smith, David Ricardo, and even Benjamin Franklin.
3. *General Theory of Employment, Interest and Money* -John Maynard Keynes
    Description: The General Theory of Employment Interest and Money is generally considered to be the masterwork of the English economist John Maynard Keynes. To a great extent it created the terminology of modern macro-economics. It was published in February 1936. The book ushered in a revolution, referred to as the "Keynesian Revolution".

Practice Test

Practice Questions

1. _____ causes a society to make tradeoffs when choosing between the production of one good or service versus another good or service.
   a. Economics
   b. Scarcity
   c. Macroeconomics
   d. Microeconomics
   e. Demand

2. Assume a society has a given production possibilities frontier (PPF) representing the production of guns and butter. Which of the following would cause the PPF to move outward?
   a. The invention of a new machine that makes guns more efficiently
   b. An increase in the production of butter
   c. An increase in the production of guns
   d. A decrease in the production of guns and butter
   e. None of the above

3. A society produces 10 units of Good X and 10 units of Good Y. Then, the society changes its production, increasing production of Good X to 15 units. Production of Good Y drops to 6 units. What is the opportunity cost of producing the additional 5 units of Good X?
   a. 5 units of Good X
   b. 15 units of Good X
   c. 6 units of Good Y
   d. 4 units of Good Y
   e. 5 units of Good X and 4 units of Good Y

4. Which of the following will result if two nations use the theory of comparative advantage when making decisions of which goods to produce and trade?
   a. Each nation will make all of their own goods
   b. Both nations will specialize in the production of the same specific goods
   c. Each nation will specialize in the production of different specific goods
   d. Neither nation will trade with one another
   e. All of the above

5. *Consider the following production possibilities for the United States and Mexico:*

Production in United States

Corn (bushels)	100	80	60	40	20	0
Oil (gallons)	0	20	40	60	80	100

Production in Mexico

Corn (bushels)	0	10	20	30	40	50
Oil (gallons)	25	20	15	10	5	0

Which of the following statements is false?
    a. The United States has an absolute advantage in corn production
    b. The United States has an absolute advantage in oil production
    c. The United States has an absolute advantage in both corn and oil production
    d. The United States has a comparative advantage in corn production
    e. The United States has a comparative advantage in oil production

6. *Consider the following production possibilities for the United States and Mexico:*

Production in United States

Corn (bushels)	100	80	60	40	20	0
Oil (gallons)	0	20	40	60	80	100

Production in Mexico

Corn (bushels)	0	10	20	30	40	50
Oil (gallons)	25	20	15	10	5	0

What should the United States do?
    a. Produce both corn and oil and trade neither with Mexico
    b. Produce both corn and oil and trade both with Mexico
    c. Produce corn and trade with Mexico for oil
    d. Produce oil and trade with Mexico for corn
    e. None of the above

7. Which of the following are true of the demand curve?
   I. It is normally downward sloping
   II. It is normally upward sloping
   III. It is influenced by the law of diminishing marginal unity
   IV. It is unaffected by the law of diminishing marginal unity
   a. I and III only
   b. I and IV only
   c. II and III only
   d. II and IV only
   e. IV only

8. Which of the following is not a part of the business cycle?
   a. Expansion
   b. Contraction
   c. Recovery
   d. Peak
   e. Stagflation

9. Which of the following correctly states a part of the Circular Flow model?
   I. Households provide inputs to the factor\ market
   II. Businesses spend money buying from the factor market
   III. Households spend money on items from the product market
   a. I only
   b. I and II only
   c. I, II, and III
   d. II and III only
   e. III only

10. Which of the following best defines American GDP?
    a. The value, in American dollars, of all goods and services produced within American borders during one calendar year
    b. The value, in American dollars, of all goods and services produced by American companies during one calendar year
    c. The total value, in American dollars, of all American household incomes during one calendar year
    d. The value, in American dollars, of a "market basket" of goods and services in one year divided by the value of the same market basket in a previous year multiplied by 100
    e. None of the above

11. The value of a "market basket" of goods and services in one year compared to the value of the same goods and services in another year is known as what?
    a. CPI
    b. GDP
    c. GNP
    d. CCI
    e. DJI

12. Which of the following is a part, or component, of GPD?
   a. GNP
   b. Consumption
   c. Supply
   d. Demand
   e. Elasticity of Demand

13. What must nominal GPD be multiplied by to arrive at real GDP?
   a. GNP
   b. CPI
   c. Supply
   d. Demand
   e. A price deflator

14. Which of the following would be included in GDP?
   a. The value of illegal drugs sold in a nation
   b. Aluminum used to make airplanes
   c. Lawn care provided by a professional nursery service
   d. Computer chips used in Apple computers
   e. All of the above

15. Which of the following could best be used in order to determine the "price deflator" for converting nominal GDP to real GDP?
   a. Consumer Price Index
   b. Gross National Product
   c. Business Cycle
   d. Phillips Curve
   e. Laffer Curve

16. In which of the following circumstances does the party in question benefit from inflation?
   a. A consumer buys a finished good
   b. A producer buys a factor (input)
   c. A person takes out a loan at a fixed interest rate
   d. A company gives out a loan at a fixed interest rate
   e. None of the above

17. Ivy loses her job because her skills as a seamstress are no longer required due to a new piece of machinery that does the work of a seamstress more quickly and for less money. Which type of unemployment is this?
   a. Frictional
   b. Structural
   c. Cyclical
   d. Careless
   e. None of the above

18. Which of the following is included in the unemployment rate typically followed by economists?

> I. Structural unemployment
> II. Frictional unemployment
> III. Cyclical unemployment

a. I only
b. II only
c. III only
d. I and II only
e. I, II, and III

19. Which is considered part of the natural rate of unemployment?

> I. Structural unemployment
> II. Frictional unemployment
> III. Cyclical unemployment

a. I only
b. II only
c. III only
d. I and II only
e. I, II, and III

20. Which of the following would not increase aggregate demand (AD)?
a. Government spending increases, while taxes stay the same
b. Consumer confidence about the economy grows
c. US government cuts defense spending dramatically while holding domestic spending steady
d. The US government cuts taxes
e. Business leaders feel economy is going to experience robust growth

21. The government increases spending by $1,000,000 and the multiplier is 5. How does this affect aggregate demand (AD)?
a. It has no effect
b. AD will increase by $5,000,000
c. AD will increase by $200,000
d. AD will decrease by $5,000,000
e. It is impossible to predict the effect

22. Assume that aggregate demand is at AD1 and the government borrows money and then spends that money in order to attempt to move aggregate demand to AD3. According to the theory of "crowding out," where is AD likely to wind up?

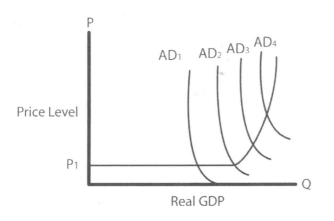

a. AD1
b. AD2
c. AD3**
d. AD4
e. Any of the above

23. Which of the following would not cause aggregate supply (AS) to change?
a. An increase or decrease in land availability
b. The labor force suddenly increases dramatically
c. A new oil discovery causes dramatic decreases in power production
d. Worker productivity remains the same
e. All of the above (no items listed above would cause AS to change)

24. How does unionized labor in an industry typically affect the wages of workers in that industry during a downturn in the economy when AD decreases?
a. It makes wages more likely to change
b. It makes wages more "sticky"
c. It has no effect on wages; instead, it causes AS to decrease
d. It has no effect on wages; instead, it causes AS to increase
e. All of the above

25. The price of oil drops dramatically, saving soda pop manufacturers great amounts of money spent on making soda pop and delivering their product to market. Prices for soda pop, however, stay the same. This is an example of what?
a. Sticky prices
b. Sticky wages
c. The multiplier effect
d. Aggregate expenditure
e. Circular flow

26. Which of the following statements about the long run aggregate supply (LRAS) curve is correct?
    a. The horizontal part represents high levels of unemployment
    b. The curved part represents high levels of unemployment
    c. The vertical part represents high levels of unemployment
    d. The LRAS curve is a straight, vertical line
    e. The LRAS curve is a straight, horizontal line

27. Assume that aggregate demand (AD) decreases. How will this decrease affect real GDP if there is a lot of unemployment as opposed to full employment?
    a. If there is a lot of unemployment, prices will rise dramatically
    b. If there is a lot of unemployment, GDP will stay the same
    c. If there is full employment, GDP will increase dramatically
    d. If there is full employment, prices will stay the same
    e. None of the above

28. The price of gasoline skyrockets, dramatically affecting the amount that producers spend to send their goods to market. What do you expect to happen in the short run?
    a. Prices increase, GDP increases
    b. Prices decrease, GDP decreases
    c. Prices increase, GDP decreases
    d. Prices decrease, GDP increases
    e. Prices stay the same, GDP stays the same

29. AD increases, leading to an increase in price levels. At the same time, GDP and unemployment stay the same. Where does the AD curve intersect the AS curve?
    a. They do not intersect
    b. In the horizontal section
    c. In the curved section
    d. In the vertical section
    e. It's impossible to say with the information given

30. Which of the following is a supply shock likely to produce?
        I. An increase in input prices
        II. An increase in price levels
        III. A decrease in employment
        IV. A decrease in GDP
    a. I and III only
    b. II and IV only
    c. I, II, and III only
    d. I, II, III, and IV
    e. None of the above

31. Which of the following is correctly defined as the total of all currency, demand deposits, money market funds, saving accounts, and CDs under $100,000?
    a. M0
    b. M1
    c. M2
    d. M3
    e. M4

32. Assume that the FOMC purchases bonds. Which of the following will happen?
    a. The money supply increases, bond yields decline, bond interest rates decline
    b. The money supply increases, bond yields increase, bond interest rates decline
    c. The money supply increases, bond yields decline, bond interest rates increase
    d. The money supply increases, bond yields increase, bond interest rates increase
    e. The money supply declines, bond yields increase, bond interest rates increase

33. Which of the following is true of money?
    a. It is a medium of exchange
    b. It is a unit of account
    c. It is a store of value
    d. It is created by a central bank
    e. All of the above

34. Which of the following statements is true of money?
               I. It is necessary for trade
               II. It is used in trade
               III. It can make trade easier
    a. I only
    b. II only
    c. III only
    d. I and II only
    e. II and III only

35. How do banks create money?
    a. By printing it
    b. By taking it out of the Federal Reserve
    c. By loaning it out
    d. By putting it into the Federal Reserve
    e. All of the above

36. Where are banks required to keep their reserves?
    a. They are not required to keep their reserves
    b. In their own vaults
    c. With the Federal Reserve
    d. With the Federal Open Market Committee
    e. In the money market

37. Sally's grandmother has kept $100,000 in a cookie jar for years and then gave it to Sally, who immediately puts it in her bank in a savings account. The bank has a 20% reserve rate. Which of the following is true?
               I. Excess reserves increase by $20,000
               II. The money supply increases by as much as $120,000
               III. Sally's grandmother was a thief
    a. I only
    b. II only
    c. I and II
    d. III
    e. None of the above

38. Which of the following would cause an increased demand for money?
    a. A decrease in the interest rate
    b. A decrease in consumer spending demand
    c. A decrease in overseas demand for domestic goods (exports)
    d. A decrease in uncertainty about future expectations
    e. None of the above

39. Which of the following correctly states the equation of exchange?
    a. $MV = PQ$
    b. $MP \times VQ$
    c. MP / VQ
    d. $VP = MQ$
    e. $1/MP = VQ$

40. What is the money multiplier if the reserve requirement is 10%?
    a. 0.1
    b. 0.01
    c. 1
    d. 10
    e. 100

41. Which of the following is true about Investment demand (Id)?
        I. The Id curve is downward sloping
        II. As interest rates increase, the amount of money demanded decreases
        III. When interest rates are high, fewer people are willing to borrow funds for investment
    a. I only
    b. II only
    c. III only
    d. I, II, and III
    e. None of the above

42. Assume that the loanable funds market is at equilibrium at the intersection of IdM1 and S. Then, the US government raises taxes on corporations. At which point is equilibrium established?

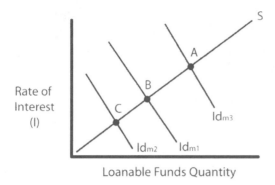

    a. A
    b. B
    c. C
    d. Some point above S
    e. None of the above

43. Which of the following is a power of the Federal Reserve?
        I. Establishing the reserve ratio requirement for banks
        II. Buy and sell Treasury Bills
        III. Set the Federal Funds Target Rate (the rate banks are charged to borrow from another bank's reserves) and the Discount Rate (the rate the Fed charges banks to borrow from the Fed)
    a. I only
    b. II only
    c. I and II only
    d. II and III only
    e. I, II, and III

44. What might the Fed do during a period with a lot of inflation?
    a. Sell Treasury Bills on the bond market
    b. Increase the Federal Funds Target Rate
    c. Increase the Discount Rate
    d. Attempt to shift the AD curve left
    e. All of the above

45. According to the quantity theory of money and the equation of exchange, what would happen to the inflation rate if V and Q were constant and the money supply increased by 5%?
   a. The rate of inflation would increase by more than 5% over the same period of time
   b. The rate of inflation would increase by 5% over the same period of time
   c. The rate of inflation would increase by less than 5% over the same period of time
   d. Inflation would not be affected
   e. It's impossible to determine what would happen to inflation

46. A business takes out a one-year loan to pay for an investment on January 1. On December 31 of that year they pay the loan back. During that time, the nation experiences a recession, and the overall price level in the economy drops. Which of the following statements is true?
   a. The nominal interest rate of the loan is greater than the real interest rate
   b. The real interest rate of the loan is greater than the nominal interest rate
   c. The nominal interest rate of the loan is greater than the nominal rate
   d. The loan has a real interest rate but not a nominal rate
   e. The loan has a nominal interest rate but not a real interest rate

47. During a recession, the government increases spending in an attempt to increase aggregate demand (AD). This is an example of what?
   a. The business cycle
   b. Fiscal policy
   c. Austrian economics
   d. Monetary policy
   e. Hyperinflation

48. During a period of inflation, the FOMC might be expected to do what?
   a. Engage in expansionary monetary policy
   b. Engage in expansionary fiscal policy
   c. Engage in contractionary monetary policy
   d. Engage in contractionary fiscal policy
   e. Increase aggregate demand (AD)

49. What might be expected to happen if the government borrows money and engages in expansionary fiscal policy that is followed by a period of "crowding out?"

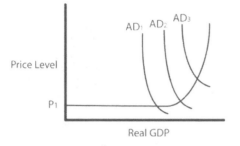

    a. AD would move from AD1 to AD2 to AD3
    b. AD would move from AD3 to AD2 to AD1
    c. AD would move from AD2 to AD1 to AD3
    d. AD would move from AD1 to AD3 to AD2
    e. AD would move from AD3 to AD1 to AD2

50. John Maynard Keynes advocated what?
    a. Supply-side economics
    b. Demand-side economics
    c. Laissez faire economics
    d. The Laffer Curve
    e. Say's Law

51. The Laffer Curve might be used to support what?
    a. Supply-side economics
    b. Demand-side economics
    c. An increase in government spending
    d. Contractionary monetary policy by the FOMC
    e. A reduction in the Discount Rate

52. Which of the following might happen if the FOMC uses Treasury Bills to pursue a contractionary monetary policy?
    a. The money supply decreases
    b. The international value of the American dollar increases
    c. The price of US goods to foreigners increases
    d. American exports drop
    e. All of the above

53. Assume a nation's economy is in recession. The nation has an MPC of 0.9 and the government wants to enact fiscal policy to shift the AD curve by $10 billion dollars. What must the government do to its current spending rate?
   a. Decrease spending by $10 billion
   b. Increase spending by $10 billion
   c. Decrease spending by $1 billion
   d. Increase spending by $1 billion
   e. Increase spending by $20 billion

54. A supply-side economist:
   I. Draws inspiration from Say's Law
   II. Believes that tax cuts increase tax revenues
   III. Believes that tax cuts leads to shifts of the AD curve to the left
   a. I only
   b. II only
   c. III only
   d. I and II only
   e. I and III only

55. Cost-push inflation might be caused by:
   I. A sudden, large increase in the cost of inputs used to make products
   II. Total spending exceeding total productivity
   III. Governments engaging in fiscal policy
   a. I only
   b. II only
   c. III only
   d. I, II, and III
   e. None of the above

56. Demand-pull inflation might be caused by:
   I. A sudden, large increase in the cost of inputs used to make products
   II. When total spending exceeds total productivity
   III. Governments engaging in fiscal policy
   a. I only
   b. II only
   c. III only
   d. I, II, and III
   e. Neither I, II, nor III

57. Hyperinflation is most likely to be associated with:
   I. Demand-pull inflation
   II. Cost-push inflation
   a. I
   b. II
   c. I and II
   d. I or II
   e. Neither I nor II

58. Inflation has what effects?
    a. Harms all members of an economy
    b. Helps all members of an economy
    c. Harms no members of an economy
    d. Helps no members of an economy
    e. Harms some members of an economy, helps others

59. Which of the following is most likely to benefit from inflation?
    a. A bond investor who owns fixed-rate bonds
    b. A retired widow with no income other than fixed Social Security payments
    c. A person who has taken out a fixed-rate loan
    d. A local bank who has loaned money out at fixed rate
    e. All of the above

60. Which of the following is true of the Phillips Curve?
    a. There is an indirect relationship between unemployment and inflation
    b. There is an indirect relationship between aggregate supply and aggregate demand
    c. There is an indirect relationship between real GDP and the consumer price index (CPI)
    d. There is an indirect relationship between fiscal policy and monetary policy
    e. There is an indirect relationship between the size of a contraction and the size of the expansion to follow in the business cycle

61. Which of the following would be most likely to try to combat inflation by decreasing the money supply?
    a. A believer in the Laffer Curve
    b. A supply-side economist
    c. A Keynesian economist
    d. An advocate of monetary policy
    e. None of the above

62. According to the Phillips Curve, an expansionary monetary policy would do what?
        I. Raise inflation
        II. Decrease unemployment
    a. I only
    b. II only
    c. I and II at the same time
    d. Either I or II (but not both)
    e. Neither I nor II

63. Which of the following is an element of the theory of rational expectations?
    a. People have no rational reason to expect monetary and fiscal policy
    b. Because people don't expect monetary and fiscal policy, they are caught unaware by it
    c. Because people are caught unaware by monetary and fiscal policy, the effects of the policy are exaggerated
    d. The lack of a rational reason to expect monetary and fiscal policy causes great swings from the natural rate of unemployment
    e. None of the above

64. Assume the Fed acts to try to keep rising prices stable. Which theory suggests that unemployment will increase as a result?
    a. Phillips curve
    b. Business cycle
    c. Circular flow model
    d. Classical economics
    e. Rational expectations

65. The occurrence of which of the following argues most directly against the theory of the Phillips Curve?
            I. Inflation
            II. Deflation
            III. Stagflation
    a. I only
    b. I and II only
    c. I and III only
    d. II and III only
    e. III only

66. How is the long-run Phillips curve different than the short-run Phillips curve?
    a. In the long-run Phillips curve, there is a trade-off between unemployment and inflation
    b. In the long-run Phillips curve, unemployment is always greater than inflation
    c. In the long-run Phillips curve, there is no trade-off between unemployment and inflation
    d. In the long-run Phillips curve, unemployment equals inflation
    e. In the long-run Phillips curve, there is no such thing as unemployment

67. Which of the following curves represents the long-run Phillips curve?

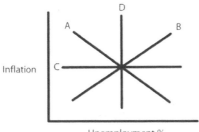

    a. A
    b. B
    c. C
    d. D
    e. None of the above

68. In the graph below, which curve (A, B, C, or D) shows the NRU of the long-run Phillips Curve?

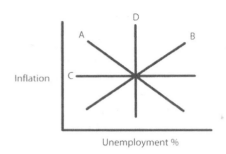

    a. A
    b. B
    c. C
    d. D
    e. It is not shown

69. In economic terms, which of the following is considered investment?
    a. Buying a new home computer
    b. Construction of a new manufacturing plant
    c. Purchase of a college education
    d. Selling finished goods to a customer
    e. All of the above

70. Which of the following is not an investment in human capital?
    a. A company hires new workers
    b. A manufacturing plant pays to teach its workers computer skills
    c. A small business gives a valued employee a raise to keep the employee with the company
    d. A film studio hires a famous actress to be in a movie
    e. All of the above are examples of investments in human capital

71. What affect might an investment in human capital be expected to have?
    a. An increase in long-run AD
    b. A decrease in long-run AD
    c. An increase in long-run AS
    d. A decrease in long-run AS
    e. None of the above

72. What affect might an investment in physical capital, through research and development, be expected to have?
    a. An increase in long-run AD
    b. A decrease in long-run AD
    c. An increase in long-run AS
    d. A decrease in long-run AS
    e. None of the above

73. The value of the goods and services exported by a country within a year and the goods and services imported by that same country during the same year is captured most directly in what?
   a. Balance of payments
   b. Current account
   c. Capital account
   d. Financial account
   e. All of the above

74. The value of a country's purchases of capital from other countries compared with the foreign purchases of capital within the country is most directly captured in what?
   a. Balance of payments
   b. Current account
   c. Capital account
   d. Financial account
   e. None of the above

75. An increase in the value of the American dollar in foreign exchange markets might be caused by what?
   a. An increase in aggregate demand (AD) in the US
   b. An increase in interest rates in the US
   c. A balance of payments that equals zero (debits equal credits)
   d. Inflation in the US
   e. A decrease in interest rates in the US

76. Country A has a current account deficit with country B. At the same time, country A has a surplus in its capital account with country B that is equal to the deficit in the current account. How would this affect the value of country A's currency in comparison with the value of country B's currency?
   a. It would have no effect; the current and capital account have nothing to do with currency values
   b. The value of the currency of country A would decrease in value
   c. The value of the currency of country A would remain the same
   d. The value of the currency of country A would increase in value
   e. The value of the currency of country A would change in an unpredictable manner

77. Assume that the exchange rate between US dollars and Canadian dollars floats freely, and that American demand for Canadian dollars decreases. What is likely to happen?
   a. Imports of American goods into Canada will increase
   b. The price of Canadian dollars in terms of American dollars will increase
   c. The price of US goods in Canadian dollars will decrease
   d. The price of Canadian goods in American dollars will increase
   e. The price of Canadian goods in American dollars will decrease

78. Assume that Guatemala has a surplus in its capital account. What might this mean?
   a. It must also have a surplus in its current account
   b. The value of Guatemalan goods bought by foreigners is greater than the value of foreign goods bought by Guatemalans
   c. Its balance of payments must be unequal
   d. The value of foreign goods bought by Guatemalans is greater than the value of Guatemalan goods bought by foreigners
   e. None of the above

79. Assume that the value of the American dollar decreases on foreign monetary currency exchanges. Which of the following is likely to happen?
   I. AS will shift right
   II. AD will shift right
   III. Inflation will result
   a. I only
   b. I and II only
   c. II and III only
   d. I, II, and III
   e. None of the above

80. A country's currency increases in value on foreign currency exchange markets. What will happen as a result?
   I. Exports will drop
   II. Imports will rise
   III. The balance of payments will rise
   a. I only
   b. II only
   c. I and II
   d. II and III
   e. III only

Answers and Explanations

1. B: Although human wants are unlimited, the number of resources in the world available to use in order to make goods and services is limited. The limited nature of resources used to make goods and services is known as scarcity. Because resources are scarce, a society cannot make all goods and services that the people in the society want. Instead, the society must choose to use the scarce resources to make a particular mix of goods and services. Choosing to make more of one good or service forces the society to make the trade-off of making less of another good or service.

2. A: The production possibilities frontier shows the different possible combinations of goods (and/or services) a society can produce. If all other factors are even, producing more of Good A leads to a decreased production of Good B. If the PPF moves outward, that means a change in the factors of production that allows the economy to produce more goods—economic growth—has occurred. Only Answer A is an example of economic growth.

3. D: Opportunity cost is a measure of what a society gives up to produce a good (or goods). When the society decides to increase its production of Good X from 10 to 15 units, it gives up the ability to produce 4 units of Good Y (with production of Good Y dropping from 10 units to 6 units). The opportunity cost of the decision, then, is 4 units of Good Y.

4. C: When a nation follows the theory of comparative advantage, it specializes in producing the goods and services it can make at a lower opportunity cost and then engages in trade to obtain other goods.

5. D: Comparative advantage is a measure of the opportunity cost of producing a good. Mexico has an opportunity cost of only 0.5 gallons of oil for each bushel of corn produced (to increase production of corn by 10 bushels, Mexico must decrease oil production by only 5 gallons). Meanwhile, the U.S. has an opportunity cost of 1 gallon of oil for each bushel of corn (to increase production of corn by 20 bushels, the U.S. must decrease oil production by 20 gallons). Mexico has a lower opportunity cost for corn production, therefore.

6. D: The United States has a comparative advantage in oil production, since their opportunity cost of producing oil is 1 bushel of corn and Mexico's opportunity cost of producing oil is 2 bushels of corn. According to the theory of comparative advantage, societies (countries) should specialize in producing goods in which they have a comparative advantage and trade for other goods. Therefore the US should produce oil and trade for corn.

7. A: As people have more and more of something, they value it less and less. This is the law of diminishing marginal utility, and it is what causes the downward slope of the demand curve.

8. E: The business cycle includes five stages: expansion, peak, contraction, trough, and recovery. Stagflation is the name for periods when inflation and unemployment are both increasing.

9. C: The circular flow model of the economy shows, in its most basic state, how inputs, goods, and money flow through the economy's four "actors": businesses, households, the factor market, and the product market. Businesses send money to the factor market in exchange for inputs, and send finished goods and services to the product market in exchange for revenue. Households send money to the product market in exchange for goods and services, and receive money from the factor market in exchange for labor and other factors.

10. A: Answer B is a definition of gross national product, and answers C and D define other economic measures.

11. A: The Consumer Price Index is the value of a "market basket" of goods and services in one year compared to the value of the same goods and services in another year.

12. B: GDP = Consumption + Investment + Government Spending + Net Exports (Exports – Imports)

13. E: Nominal GDP is the total dollar value of goods and services produced in a country in a year. However, since prices increase with inflation, nominal GDP gives a skewed view of an economy when looking at various years over time. Therefore, economists multiply nominal GDP by a price deflator that accounts for inflation in order to arrive at real GDP.

14. C: GDP measures only the value of final goods and services provided in a nation. The value of inputs—such as aluminum or computer chips—is not included, nor is the value of illegally sold goods and services such as illicit drugs.

15. A: Converting nominal GDP to real GDP requires some measure of the change in prices of goods and services within a nation over time. One could use the Consumer Price Index—the value of a fixed "market basket" of goods and services on a yearly basis—to determine the rate of inflation and then adjust nominal GDP to real GDP.

16. C: When a person takes out a loan at a fixed interest rate, and then the society experiences inflation, the inflation effectively reduces or wipes out the interest paid. For example, if a person takes out a loan at 5 percent interest, and during that time the inflation rate is 5 percent, the person has essentially taken out an interest-free loan. In the other circumstances listed, the people do feel a cost from inflation.

17. B: Structural unemployment is unemployment that results from a mismatch of job skills or location. In this case, Ivy's job skill—her ability to work as a seamstress—is no longer desired by employers. Frictional and cyclical are other forms of unemployment; economists do not use the term careless unemployment.

18. C: Economists are interested in unemployment caused by changes in the business cycle. That is what cyclical unemployment measures. There will always be some measure of structural and frictional unemployment, and those are not typically considered when assessing the unemployment picture in a nation.

19. D: It is believed that some level of frictional and structural unemployment will always exist, and that the best economists (and politicians) can hope for is to reduce cyclical unemployment to zero. Therefore, frictional and structural unemployment are sometimes

referred to as natural unemployment, meaning unemployment that naturally exists within an economy.

20. C: If the government cuts defense spending but does not shift that money to other spending, that will have a negative effect on AD, causing AD to decrease. All of the other options would increase AD.

21. B: The multiplier effect states that a given increase in spending, when multiplied by the multiplier, will lead to a given increase in AD. In this case, the $1,000,000 spending increase and the multiplier of 5 lead to an AD increase of $5,000,000 ($1,000,000 x 5 = $5,000,000).

22. B: According to the theory of crowding out, when the government borrows money to increase spending, this will increase the price of money, leading to a drop in investment. That drop in investment will have a negative effect on AD, and so the government injection of funds will not have its full, desired effect (AD3), instead winding up at AD2.

23. D: A change in productivity, such as workers becoming more or less productive, would affect how many goods can be supplied. No change in worker productivity would cause no change in AS. Items A, B, and C would all affect input prices and therefore would all affect AS.

24. B: When AD for the goods produced by an industry decreases, one might expect the wages paid to workers in that industry to decrease as a result. However, because unions negotiate contracts with employers, wages of unionized workers tend not to fall in these circumstances. This tendency to for wages to stay the same is known as "sticky wages."

25. A: The phenomenon of "sticky prices" refers to prices that stay the same even though it seems they should change (either increasing or decreasing).

26. D: In the long run, aggregate supply does not depend on price. Aggregate supply in the long run depends strictly on the amount of capital and labor and the type of available technology.

27. E: When there is a lot of unemployment, the AS curve is horizontal. If AD decreases at this time, prices will tend to remain the same while GDP decreases. When there is full employment, the AS curve is vertical. If AD decreases at this time, prices will drop but GDP will tend to remain the same.

28. C: The increased cost of gasoline increases the cost of transportation. This is a variable cost of supply, and so the AS curve shifts inward and upward. In the short run, AD would remain fixed, leading to a rise in prices and decreased GDP.

29. D: If AD rises do not lead to an increase in GDP, the AD curve must intersect the AS curve in the vertical section of the AS curve, when employment is full. Such a situation leads to extremes of inflation.

30. D: A supply shock is caused when there is a dramatic increase in input prices. This causes an increase in price levels and decreases in employment and GDP. A supply shock causes the AS curve to move to the left (in).

31. B: There are several different measures of the national money supply; these include M1, M2, and M3; there is no M4. M1 is defined as the total of all currency, demand deposits, money market funds, saving accounts, and CDs under $100,000.

32. D: When the FOMC purchases bonds, that brings an increase to the money supply, and there is an increase in bond yields and bond interest rates. When the FOMC sells bonds, that decreases the money supply, and bond yields and bond interest rates go down.

33. E: Money, which can be created by the central bank, is defined as a. a medium of exchange, b. a unit of account, c. a store of value, and d. sometimes, a standard of deferred payment.

34. E: Money can be used in trade and can make trade easier, but it is not necessary for trade, as people can barter for goods and services.

35. C: Banks create money by giving out loans. For example, assume a person puts $100 into a bank. The bank will keep a percentage of that money in reserves because of the reserve requirement. If the reserve requirement is 10% then the bank will put $10 in reserves and then loan out $90 of it to a second person. The money total, which started at $100, now includes the original $100 plus the $90, or a total of $190. The bank creates $90 by loaning it.

36. C: Banks are required to keep a particular percentage of their money on deposit with the Federal Reserve. These are deposits that the banks cannot lend. These requirements affect the bank's ability to create money (affecting the total amount a bank can loan) and are part of the Fed's toolkit for monetary policy.

37. E: None of the options listed are true (and we do not know if Sally's grandmother was a thief). Excess reserves will increase by $80,000, as the bank must keep 20% of the deposit, or $20,000, leaving $80,000. The money multiplier is 1/Reserve ratio, or 5, and that means the money supply could increase a total of $500,000--$100,000 + (5 x $80,000).

38. A: A decrease in the interest rate would increase demand for money, as more people want to get out of investments. The other items listed would cause a decrease in demand for money.

39. A: The equation of exchange is MV = PQ. This means that M1 (a measure of the supply of money) multiplied by the velocity of money (the average number of times a typical dollar is spent on final goods and services a year) = the average price level of final goods and services in GDP x real output, or the quantity of goods and services in GDP.

40. D: To determine the money multiplier, use the formula MM (money multiplier) = 1/Reserve Ratio (RR). In this case, that's MM = 1/ (1/10), or 10.

41. D: All three statements are different ways to saying the same thing—when interest rates for investment are high, few people want to take out loans.

42. C: When the government increases taxes on corporations, it lowers their willingness to invest—represented by the Id curve. That means that the Idm1 curve will move to Idm2, with a new equilibrium of C.

- 103 -

43. E: The Fed's ability to set the reserve ratio requirement for banks is the foundation of fractional reserve banking. The Fed's ability to buy and sell Treasury Bills in the bond market, called monetary policy, is the Fed's most effective way to affect the money supply. And the Fed can establish both the Federal Funds Target Rate and the Discount Rate.

44. E: During a period of inflation, the Fed's goal would be to slow down the economy. To do this, it would sell Treasury Bills on the bond market to remove money from the economy (option A), and increase the Federal Funds Rate and Discount Rate to make it harder for money to change hands (options B and C). These actions would serve to shift the AD curve to the left (option D).

45. B: If V and Q are constant, any change to P must equal any change to M, meaning that the rate of inflation would equal the growth of the money supply.

46. A: The nominal interest rate is stated interest rate, while the real interest rate is the nominal interest rate adjusted for inflation. If prices decrease during the period of the loan, the real interest rate will be less than the nominal interest rate.

47. B: When a government spends money or collects revenues (in the form taxes) in an attempt to influence the economy's performance, it is known as fiscal policy.

48. C: The Federal Open Market Committee (FOMC), part of the Federal Reserve, only has the ability to perform monetary policy, not fiscal policy. Monetary policy affects the supply of money in the economy when the FOMC buys or sells Treasury bills or changes interest rates. In a period of high inflation, the FOMC might try to counter this by reducing the supply of money. This would be an example of contractionary monetary policy.

49. D: If the government engages in expansionary fiscal policy, aggregate demand would rise. The government would have to borrow money, however, to increase its spending. This would raise interest rates, which might cause businesses to invest more, leading to a resulting decrease in AD. This is best captured by the movement of AD from AD1 to AD3 to AD2.

50. B: John Maynard Keynes argued that government could help revitalize a recessionary economy by increasing government spending and therefore increasing aggregate demand. This is known as demand-side economics.

51. A: The Laffer Curve, a theoretical construction, shows the relationship between government tax rates and total government revenue, and claims that as government tax rates increase after a certain point, total tax revenues decrease. Supply-side economists sometimes use the Laffer Curve to argue against classical Keynesian demand-side economics, arguing instead for lower tax rates. They argue that increased spending by businesses will lead to increased welfare, and that supply will create its own demand.

52. E: When the FOMC sells bonds, they raise interest rates. This draws money out of the American economy, and attracts foreign investors. This causes the value of the American dollar to rise overseas, which makes American goods more expensive to overseas buyers and causes American exports to drop.

53. D: Because the MPC is 0.9, the multiplier is 10 (1/0.1). Therefore, to attain an increase of $10 billion in AD, the government must increase spending by $1 billion ($1 billion x 10 = $10 billion).

54. D: Supply-side economists believe that supply creates demand. This is Say's Law. They also believe that tax cuts increase tax revenue. This is illustrated in the Laffer Curve. Finally, they believe that tax cuts will lead to a rightward shift of the AD curve.

55. A: Cost-push inflation is caused when the price of a resource rises dramatically and unexpectedly. This is sometimes known as a "supply shock." A classic example is the supply shock experienced in the US during the 1970s when the price of oil dramatically increased.

56. B: Demand-pull inflation is caused when spending exceeds production. The "excess" demand drives up prices of goods.

57. A: Demand-pull inflation is caused when total spending is in excess of total production. This causes price levels to rise, and can lead to hyperinflation.

58. E: While rising prices may hurt many members of an economy, those same rising prices may benefit other members of the same economy. For example, rising prices may help those who sell goods and services and are able to keep their costs of production low, increasing their profit margin. Meanwhile, rising prices can hurt consumers because their income is now able to purchase fewer goods and services than before.

59. C: A person who has taken out a fixed-rate loan can benefit from inflation by paying back the loan with dollars that are less valuable than they were when the loan was taken out. In the other examples, inflation harms the individual or entity.

60. A: According to the Phillips Curve, as stated by British economist A.W. Phillips in 1958, inflation and unemployment have an inverse relationship, meaning one is high when the other is low, and vice versa.

61. D: Monetary policy is the practice of shrinking and growing the money supply in order to combat inflation and/or deflation and otherwise attempt to "adjust" the economy.

62. C: The Phillips curve states that there is an inverse relationship between inflation and unemployment. An expansionary monetary policy would cause inflation to rise. According to the Phillips Curve, then, this increase in inflation would be joined by a decrease in unemployment.

63. E: According to the theory of rational expectations, people adjust their actions as a result of rational expectations of fiscal and monetary policy. The adjusted actions reduce the effects of the fiscal or monetary policy, and move the economy toward a natural rate of unemployment.

64. A: The Phillips Curve says that inflation and unemployment have an indirect relationship. If the Fed acts to stop inflation, then according to the Phillips Curve, unemployment will increase.

65. E: According to the Phillips Curve, when inflation is high, unemployment is low, and when inflation is low, unemployment is high. In stagflation, both inflation and unemployment are high.

66. C: In the short-run Phillips curve, there is a trade-off between unemployment and inflation. There is no such trade-off in the long-run Phillips curve. According to the long-run Phillips curve, the economy tends to stay at the natural rate of unemployment, and any changes are minor variations that will self-correct.

67. D: In the long-run Phillips Curve, unemployment stays at the natural rate of unemployment (NRU). As a result, while price levels change increase and decrease, movement along the long-run Phillips Curve is only up or down.

68. D: The long-run Phillips curve is a vertical line at the natural rate of unemployment. That's because according to the long-run Phillips curve, there is no trade-off between inflation and unemployment in the long run. Instead, the economy tends to self-correct to a natural rate of unemployment.

69. B: Any expenditure that will increase a firm's future productivity is considered investment. Of the items listed, only the construction of a new plant matches the definition.

70. E: Human capital is the labor that businesses use to make products. All of the examples listed are expenditures to secure human capital in order to products (good or services).

71. C: An investment in any type of capital, assuming all else stays the same, is likely to lead to an increase in long-run aggregate supply.

72. C: An investment in any type of capital, assuming all else stays the same, is likely to lead to an increase in long-run aggregate supply.

73. B: The current account is part of what makes up a country's balance of payment account. The current account records the value of exports and imports of goods and services by a country, the country's net investment income, and the country's net transfers.

74. C: The capital account is part of what makes up a country's balance of payments account. The capital account compares the amount of foreign capital bought by a country with the amount of the same country's capital bought by foreigners.

75. B: If interest rates in the US increase, foreign investors may send more money to the US. Those investors would have to first exchange their currencies for American dollars, making the American dollars more valued (scarce) and therefore increase in value.

76. C: Country A has a deficit with country B in the current account. On its own, that would tend to reduce the value of country A's currency when compared with country B. However, the current account deficit is balance out by the capital account's surplus, leaving the value of the currency unchanged.

77. E: When demand for a foreign currency drops, the value of that currency drops. This makes it cheaper to buy goods from that foreign country.

78. B: The current account is a measurement of a country's net exports. If a country has a current account surplus, the value of the goods and services it is exporting is greater than the value of the goods and services it is importing.

79. C: If the value of the American dollar decreases, American goods will be cheaper for foreign buyers, causing AD to shift right. This will lead to inflation.

80. C: If a country's currency increases in value, foreigners will have to give up more of their own currency to get the original country's currency in order to buy the original country's goods and services. This will cause a drop in exports. At the same time, it will be less expensive for people in the original country to exchange their currency for foreign currencies, causing the price of imported goods to drop and the total value of imports to rise.

Secret Key #1 - Time is Your Greatest Enemy

Pace Yourself

Wear a watch. At the beginning of the test, check the time (or start a chronometer on your watch to count the minutes), and check the time after each passage or every few questions to make sure you are "on schedule."

If you are forced to speed up, do it efficiently. Usually one or more answer choices can be eliminated without too much difficulty. Above all, don't panic. Don't speed up and just begin guessing at random choices. By pacing yourself, and continually monitoring your progress against your watch, you will always know exactly how far ahead or behind you are with your available time. If you find that you are one minute behind on the test, don't skip one question without spending any time on it, just to catch back up. Take 15 fewer seconds on the next four questions, and after four questions you'll have caught back up. Once you catch back up, you can continue working each problem at your normal pace.

Furthermore, don't dwell on the problems that you were rushed on. If a problem was taking up too much time and you made a hurried guess, it must be difficult. The difficult questions are the ones you are most likely to miss anyway, so it isn't a big loss. It is better to end with more time than you need than to run out of time.

Lastly, sometimes it is beneficial to slow down if you are constantly getting ahead of time. You are always more likely to catch a careless mistake by working more slowly than quickly, and among very high-scoring test takers (those who are likely to have lots of time left over), careless errors affect the score more than mastery of material.

Secret Key #2 - Guessing is not Guesswork

You probably know that guessing is a good idea - unlike other standardized tests, there is no penalty for getting a wrong answer. Even if you have no idea about a question, you still have a 20-25% chance of getting it right.

Most test takers do not understand the impact that proper guessing can have on their score. Unless you score extremely high, guessing will significantly contribute to your final score.

Monkeys Take the Test

What most test takers don't realize is that to insure that 20-25% chance, you have to guess randomly. If you put 20 monkeys in a room to take this test, assuming they answered once per question and behaved themselves, on average they would get 20-25% of the questions correct. Put 20 test takers in the room, and the average will be much lower among guessed questions. Why?
   1. The test writers intentionally writes deceptive answer choices that "look" right. A test taker has no idea about a question, so picks the "best looking" answer, which is

often wrong. The monkey has no idea what looks good and what doesn't, so will consistently be lucky about 20-25% of the time.
2. Test takers will eliminate answer choices from the guessing pool based on a hunch or intuition. Simple but correct answers often get excluded, leaving a 0% chance of being correct. The monkey has no clue, and often gets lucky with the best choice.

This is why the process of elimination endorsed by most test courses is flawed and detrimental to your performance- test takers don't guess, they make an ignorant stab in the dark that is usually worse than random.

$5 Challenge

Let me introduce one of the most valuable ideas of this course- the $5 challenge:

You only mark your "best guess" if you are willing to bet $5 on it.
You only eliminate choices from guessing if you are willing to bet $5 on it.

Why $5? Five dollars is an amount of money that is small yet not insignificant, and can really add up fast (20 questions could cost you $100). Likewise, each answer choice on one question of the test will have a small impact on your overall score, but it can really add up to a lot of points in the end.

The process of elimination IS valuable. The following shows your chance of guessing it right:

If you eliminate wrong answer choices until only this many remain:	Chance of getting it correct:
1	100%
2	50%
3	33%

However, if you accidentally eliminate the right answer or go on a hunch for an incorrect answer, your chances drop dramatically: to 0%. By guessing among all the answer choices, you are GUARANTEED to have a shot at the right answer.

That's why the $5 test is so valuable- if you give up the advantage and safety of a pure guess, it had better be worth the risk.

What we still haven't covered is how to be sure that whatever guess you make is truly random. Here's the easiest way:

Always pick the first answer choice among those remaining.

Such a technique means that you have decided, **before you see a single test question**, exactly how you are going to guess- and since the order of choices tells you nothing about which one is correct, this guessing technique is perfectly random.

This section is not meant to scare you away from making educated guesses or eliminating choices- you just need to define when a choice is worth eliminating. The $5 test, along with a pre-defined random guessing strategy, is the best way to make sure you reap all of the benefits of guessing.

Secret Key #3 - Practice Smarter, Not Harder

Many test takers delay the test preparation process because they dread the awful amounts of practice time they think necessary to succeed on the test. We have refined an effective method that will take you only a fraction of the time.
There are a number of "obstacles" in your way to succeed. Among these are answering questions, finishing in time, and mastering test-taking strategies. All must be executed on the day of the test at peak performance, or your score will suffer. The test is a mental marathon that has a large impact on your future.

Just like a marathon runner, it is important to work your way up to the full challenge. So first you just worry about questions, and then time, and finally strategy:

Success Strategy

1. Find a good source for practice tests.
2. If you are willing to make a larger time investment, consider using more than one study guide- often the different approaches of multiple authors will help you "get" difficult concepts.
3. Take a practice test with no time constraints, with all study helps "open book." Take your time with questions and focus on applying strategies.
4. Take a practice test with time constraints, with all guides "open book."
5. Take a final practice test with no open material and time limits

If you have time to take more practice tests, just repeat step 5. By gradually exposing yourself to the full rigors of the test environment, you will condition your mind to the stress of test day and maximize your success.

Secret Key #4 - Prepare, Don't Procrastinate

Let me state an obvious fact: if you take the test three times, you will get three different scores. This is due to the way you feel on test day, the level of preparedness you have, and, despite the test writers' claims to the contrary, some tests WILL be easier for you than others.
Since your future depends so much on your score, you should maximize your chances of success. In order to maximize the likelihood of success, you've got to prepare in advance. This means taking practice tests and spending time learning the information and test taking strategies you will need to succeed.

Since you have to pay a registration fee each time you take the test, don't take it as a "practice" test. Feel free to take sample tests on your own, but when you go to take the official test, be prepared, be focused, and do your best the first time!

Secret Key #5 - Test Yourself

Everyone knows that time is money. There is no need to spend too much of your time or too little of your time preparing for the test. You should only spend as much of your precious time preparing as is necessary for you to pass it.

Once you have taken a practice test under real conditions of time constraints, then you will know if you are ready for the test or not.

If you have scored extremely high the first time that you take the practice test, then there is not much point in spending countless hours studying. You are already there.

Benchmark your abilities by retaking practice tests and seeing how much you have improved. Once you score high enough to guarantee success, then you are ready.

If you have scored well below where you need, then knuckle down and begin studying in earnest. Check your improvement regularly through the use of practice tests under real conditions. Above all, don't worry, panic, or give up. The key is perseverance!

Then, when you go to take the test, remain confident and remember how well you did on the practice tests. If you can score high enough on a practice test, then you can do the same on the real thing.

General Strategies

The most important thing you can do is to ignore your fears and jump into the test immediately- do not be overwhelmed by any strange-sounding terms. You have to jump into the test like jumping into a pool- all at once is the easiest way.

Make Predictions
As you read and understand the question, try to guess what the answer will be. Remember that several of the answer choices are wrong, and once you begin reading them, your mind will immediately become cluttered with answer choices designed to throw you off. Your mind is typically the most focused immediately after you have read the passage and question and digested its contents. If you can, try to predict what the correct answer will be. You may be surprised at what you can predict.

Quickly scan the choices and see if your prediction is in the listed answer choices. If it is, then you can be quite confident that you have the right answer. It still won't hurt to check the other answer choices, but most of the time, you've got it!

Answer the Question
It may seem obvious to only pick answer choices that answer the question, but the test writers can create some excellent answer choices that are wrong. Don't pick an answer just because it sounds right, or you believe it to be true. It MUST answer the question. Once you've made your selection, always go back and check it against the question and make sure that you didn't misread the question, and the answer choice does answer the question posed.

Benchmark

After you read the first answer choice, decide if you think it sounds correct or not. If it doesn't, move on to the next answer choice. If it does, tentatively check that answer choice. This doesn't mean that you've definitely selected it as your answer choice, it just means that it's the best you've seen thus far. Go ahead and read the next choice. If the next choice is worse than the one you've already selected, keep going to the next answer choice. If the next choice is better than the choice you've already selected, check the new answer choice as your best guess.

The first answer choice that you select becomes your standard. Every other answer choice must be benchmarked against that standard. That choice is correct until proven otherwise by another answer choice beating it out. Once you've decided that no other answer choice seems as good, do one final check to ensure that your answer choice answers the question posed.

Valid Information

Don't discount any of the information provided in the question. Every piece of information may be necessary to determine the correct answer. None of the information in the question is there to throw you off (while the answer choices will certainly have information to throw you off). If two seemingly unrelated topics are discussed, don't ignore either. You can be confident there is a relationship, or it wouldn't be included in the question, and you are probably going to have to determine what is that relationship for the answer.

Avoid "Fact Traps"

Don't get distracted by a choice that is factually true. Your search is for the answer that answers the question. Stay focused and don't fall for an answer that is true but incorrect. Always go back to the question and make sure you're choosing an answer that actually answers the question and is not just a true statement. An answer can be factually correct, but it MUST answer the question asked. Additionally, two answers can both be seemingly correct, so be sure to read all of the answer choices, and make sure that you get the one that BEST answers the question.

Milk the Question

Some of the questions may throw you completely off. They might deal with a subject you have not been exposed to, or one that you haven't reviewed in years. While your lack of knowledge about the subject will be a hindrance, the question itself can give you many clues that will help you find the correct answer. Read the question carefully, and look for clues. Watch particularly for adjectives and nouns describing difficult terms or words that you don't recognize. Regardless of if you understand a word or not, replacing it with the synonyms used for it in the question may help you to understand what the questions are asking.

Look carefully for these descriptive synonyms (nouns) and adjectives and use them to help you understand the difficult terms. Rather than wracking your mind about specific detail information concerning a difficult term in the question, use the more general description or synonym provided to make it easier for you.

The Trap of Familiarity

Don't just choose a word because you recognize it. On difficult questions, you may not recognize a number of words in the answer choices. The test writers don't put "make-believe" words on the test; so don't think that just because you only recognize all the words in one answer choice means that answer choice must be correct. If you don't recognize

- 112 -

words in all but one answer choices, then focus on the one that you do recognize. Is it correct? Try your best to determine if it is correct. If it does, that is great, but if it doesn't, eliminate it. Each word and answer choice you eliminate increases your chances of getting the question correct, even if you then have to guess among the unfamiliar choices.

Eliminate Answers

Eliminate choices as soon as you realize they are wrong. But be careful! Make sure you consider all of the possible answer choices. Just because one appears right, doesn't mean that the next one won't be even better! The test writers will usually put more than one good answer choice for every question, so read all of them. Don't worry if you are stuck between two that seem right. By getting down to just two remaining possible choices, your odds are now 50/50. Rather than wasting too much time, play the odds. You are guessing, but guessing wisely, because you've been able to knock out some of the answer choices that you know are wrong. If you are eliminating choices and realize that the last answer choice you are left with is also obviously wrong, don't panic. Start over and consider each choice again. There may easily be something that you missed the first time and will realize on the second pass.

Tough Questions

If you are stumped on a problem or it appears too hard or too difficult, don't waste time. Move on! Remember though, if you can quickly check for obviously incorrect answer choices, your chances of guessing correctly are greatly improved. Before you completely give up, at least try to knock out a couple of possible answers. Eliminate what you can and then guess at the remaining answer choices before moving on.

Brainstorm

If you get stuck on a difficult question, spend a few seconds quickly brainstorming. Run through the complete list of possible answer choices. Look at each choice and ask yourself, "Could this answer the question satisfactorily?" Go through each answer choice and consider it independently of the other. By systematically going through all possibilities, you may find something that you would otherwise overlook. Remember that when you get stuck, it's important to try to keep moving.

Read Carefully

Understand the problem. Read the question and answer choices carefully. Don't miss the question because you misread the terms. You have plenty of time to read each question thoroughly and make sure you understand what is being asked. Yet a happy medium must be attained, so don't waste too much time. You must read carefully, but efficiently.

Face Value

When in doubt, use common sense. Always accept the situation in the problem at face value. Don't read too much into it. These problems will not require you to make huge leaps of logic. The test writers aren't trying to throw you off with a cheap trick. If you have to go beyond creativity and make a leap of logic in order to have an answer choice answer the question, then you should look at the other answer choices. Don't overcomplicate the problem by creating theoretical relationships or explanations that will warp time or space. These are normal problems rooted in reality. It's just that the applicable relationship or explanation may not be readily apparent and you have to figure things out. Use your common sense to interpret anything that isn't clear.

Prefixes

If you're having trouble with a word in the question or answer choices, try dissecting it. Take advantage of every clue that the word might include. Prefixes and suffixes can be a huge help. Usually they allow you to determine a basic meaning. Pre- means before, post- means after, pro - is positive, de- is negative. From these prefixes and suffixes, you can get an idea of the general meaning of the word and try to put it into context. Beware though of any traps. Just because con is the opposite of pro, doesn't necessarily mean congress is the opposite of progress!

Hedge Phrases

Watch out for critical "hedge" phrases, such as likely, may, can, will often, sometimes, etc, often, almost, mostly, usually, generally, rarely, sometimes. Question writers insert these hedge phrases to cover every possibility. Often an answer choice will be wrong simply because it leaves no room for exception. Avoid answer choices that have definitive words like "exactly," and "always".

Switchback Words

Stay alert for "switchbacks". These are the words and phrases frequently used to alert you to shifts in thought. The most common switchback word is "but". Others include although, however, nevertheless, on the other hand, even though, while, in spite of, despite, regardless of.

New Information

Correct answer choices will rarely have completely new information included. Answer choices typically are straightforward reflections of the material asked about and will directly relate to the question. If a new piece of information is included in an answer choice that doesn't even seem to relate to the topic being asked about, then that answer choice is likely incorrect. All of the information needed to answer the question is usually provided for you, and so you should not have to make guesses that are unsupported or choose answer choices that require unknown information that cannot be reasoned on its own.

Time Management

On technical questions, don't get lost on the technical terms. Don't spend too much time on any one question. If you don't know what a term means, then since you don't have a dictionary, odds are you aren't going to get much further. You should immediately recognize terms as whether or not you know them. If you don't, work with the other clues that you have, the other answer choices and terms provided, but don't waste too much time trying to figure out a difficult term.

Contextual Clues

Look for contextual clues. An answer can be right but not correct. The contextual clues will help you find the answer that is most right and is correct. Understand the context in which a phrase is stated. This will help you make important distinctions.

Don't Panic

Panicking will not answer any questions for you. Therefore, it isn't helpful. When you first see the question, if your mind goes blank, take a deep breath. Force yourself to mechanically go through the steps of solving the problem and using the strategies you've learned.

Pace Yourself

Don't get clock fever. It's easy to be overwhelmed when you're looking at a page full of questions, your mind is full of random thoughts and feeling confused, and the clock is ticking down faster than you would like. Calm down and maintain the pace that you have set for yourself. As long as you are on track by monitoring your pace, you are guaranteed to have enough time for yourself. When you get to the last few minutes of the test, it may seem like you won't have enough time left, but if you only have as many questions as you should have left at that point, then you're right on track!

Answer Selection

The best way to pick an answer choice is to eliminate all of those that are wrong, until only one is left and confirm that is the correct answer. Sometimes though, an answer choice may immediately look right. Be careful! Take a second to make sure that the other choices are not equally obvious. Don't make a hasty mistake. There are only two times that you should stop before checking other answers. First is when you are positive that the answer choice you have selected is correct. Second is when time is almost out and you have to make a quick guess!

Check Your Work

Since you will probably not know every term listed and the answer to every question, it is important that you get credit for the ones that you do know. Don't miss any questions through careless mistakes. If at all possible, try to take a second to look back over your answer selection and make sure you've selected the correct answer choice and haven't made a costly careless mistake (such as marking an answer choice that you didn't mean to mark). This quick double check should more than pay for itself in caught mistakes for the time it costs.

Beware of Directly Quoted Answers

Sometimes an answer choice will repeat word for word a portion of the question or reference section. However, beware of such exact duplication – it may be a trap! More than likely, the correct choice will paraphrase or summarize a point, rather than being exactly the same wording.

Slang

Scientific sounding answers are better than slang ones. An answer choice that begins "To compare the outcomes…" is much more likely to be correct than one that begins "Because some people insisted…"

Extreme Statements

Avoid wild answers that throw out highly controversial ideas that are proclaimed as established fact. An answer choice that states the "process should be used in certain situations, if…" is much more likely to be correct than one that states the "process should be discontinued completely." The first is a calm rational statement and doesn't even make a definitive, uncompromising stance, using a hedge word "if" to provide wiggle room, whereas the second choice is a radical idea and far more extreme.

Answer Choice Families

When you have two or more answer choices that are direct opposites or parallels, one of them is usually the correct answer. For instance, if one answer choice states "x increases" and another answer choice states "x decreases" or "y increases," then those two or three answer choices are very similar in construction and fall into the same family of answer choices. A family of answer choices is when two or three answer choices are very similar in construction, and yet often have a directly opposite meaning. Usually the correct answer choice will be in that family of answer choices. The "odd man out" or answer choice that doesn't seem to fit the parallel construction of the other answer choices is more likely to be incorrect.

Special Report: Additional Bonus Material

Due to our efforts to try to keep this book to a manageable length, we've created a link that will give you access to all of your additional bonus material.

Please visit http://www.mometrix.com/bonus948/clepprimacroec to access the information.